Jackaroo

fantastical pieces for absolute beginners

Caroline Lumsden and **Pam Wedgwood**

with illustrations by **Drew Hillier**

Contents

FABER *ff* MUSIC

Foreword

I hope you have as much fun playing these pieces as Pam and I had in the writing of them. Feel free to make them your own by adding second verse words where needed, inventing a new noise on the instrument, or trying out different dynamics. There's even space for you to create your own imaginary animals!

Caroline Lumsden

I really enjoyed drawing these pictures for you, but now it's YOUR turn to have fun and let your imagination run ... WWWWWILD! So go on, grab some pencils and fill the landscapes with your own imaginary creatures—but don't forget to play your viola too!

Drew Hillier

First published in 2002 by Faber Music Ltd
3 Queen Square London WC1N 3AU
Music processed by MusicSet 2000
Printed in England by Caligraving Ltd

ISBN 0-571-52169-X

To buy Faber Music publications or to find out about the full range of titles available please contact your local music retailer or Faber Music sales enquiries:

Faber Music Limited, Burnt Mill,
Elizabeth Way, Harlow, CM20 2HX England
Tel: +44 (0)1279 82 89 82 Fax: +44 (0)1279 82 89 83
sales@fabermusic.com fabermusic.com

on an idea by Jim

Pizz. = Pizzicato (pluck string with first finger)
[windmill symbol] = Make a circle in the air with the bow
> = Accent
[pause symbol] = Pause
[pencil symbol] Try making up words for a second verse

Zebraphants March

on an idea by Olivia

ACTION March as you play; stamp for the last three notes
Cresc. = Crescendo (getting gradually louder)
Poco rit. = Poco ritenuto (held back)

Crocodillo Snap

on an idea by Harry

⚲ = *Snap pizz. (pull string quickly and let it rebound)*

Snappily, at middle of bow ♩ = 54

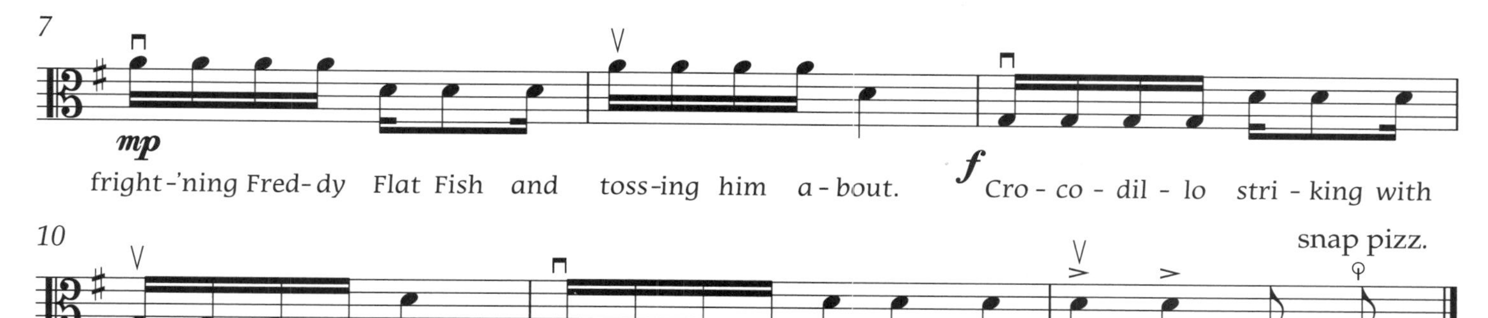

Lazy Chimliroo

on an idea by Harry

Lazily, sway freely ♩ = 88

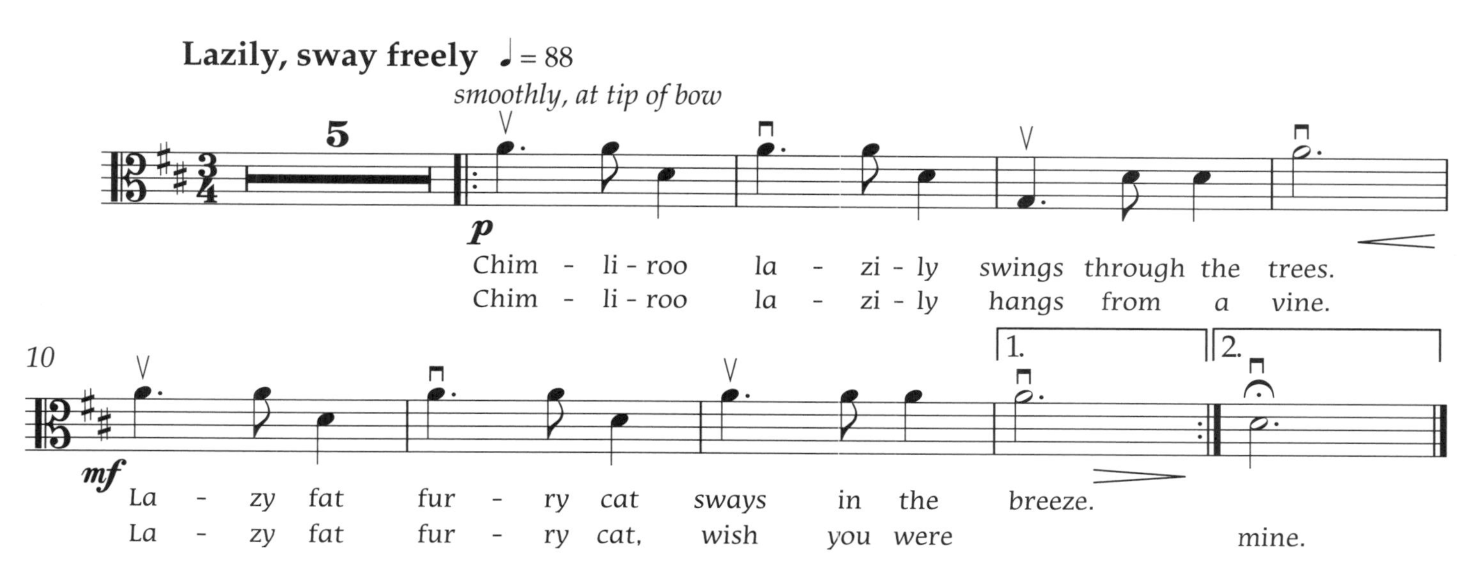

What sort of animals
do you think these are?

____

____

Henpecker

on an idea by Katy

Col legno = Tip bow over onto the wood and let it bounce

(rocket symbol) = Push bowing arm straight up into the air

Jazzy, with a good swing ♩ = 116 – 120

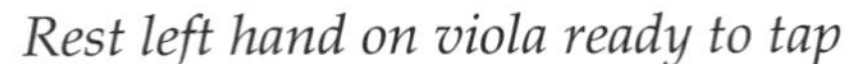

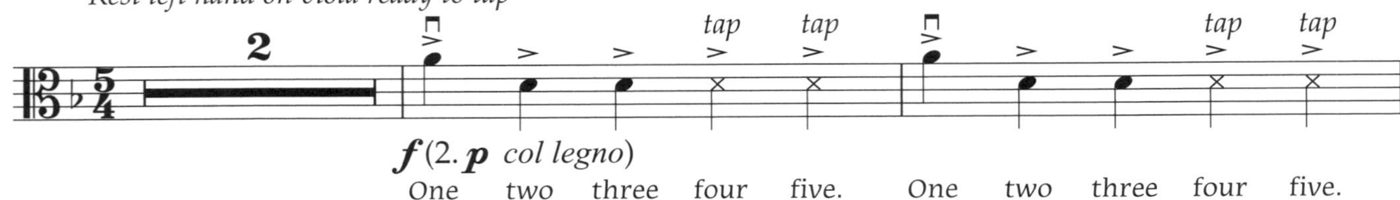

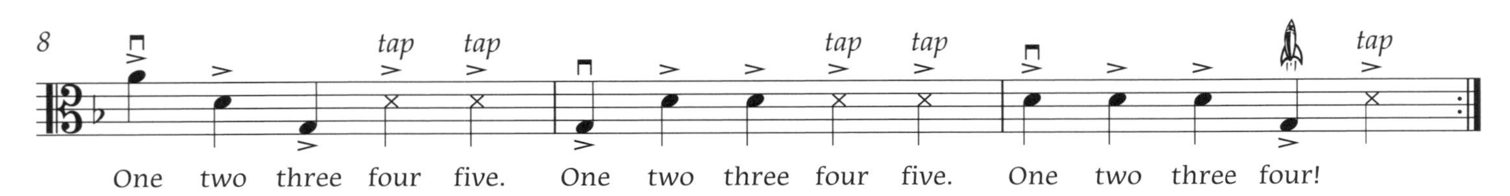

Imaginary Animal 1

ACTION Listen to your teacher play, then it's your turn to copy!

Don't forget to give this new creature a name. You can even draw it in the space below!

My new animal is called a ______________________________

Humming Cat

𝄞 = Treble clef (your teacher will explain this)

° = Harmonic (your teacher will show you how to play this)

ACTION Ask your audience to join in the 'miaow'!

Cat-like and peaceful ♩ = 84

Imaginary Animal 2

This animal is called a

____

VIOLA and PIANO

fantastical pieces for absolute beginners

Caroline Lumsden and **Pam Wedgwood**

with illustrations by **Drew Hillier**

Contents

First published in 2002 by Faber Music Ltd
3 Queen Square London WC1N 3AU
Music processed by MusicSet 2000
Printed in England by Caligraving Ltd

ISBN 0-571-52169-X

To buy Faber Music publications or to find out about the full range of titles available please contact your local music retailer or Faber Music sales enquiries:

Faber Music Limited, Burnt Mill, Elizabeth Way, Harlow, CM20 2HX England
Tel: +44 (0)1279 82 89 82 Fax: +44 (0)1279 82 89 83
sales@fabermusic.com fabermusic.com

Foreword

Jackaroo *was inspired by pupils of the Beauchamp Music Group, Gloucester.*

Each piece introduces a new rhythmic or technical point and the addition of words means that all the pieces can be sung through first with the piano. Teaching points and a suggestion box for learning each new piece are given in the score—you may find the following formula a useful way to tackle each new piece:

1. *Sing through once with the words*
2. *Sing and clap with the time names e.g. Py-thon-ip-po-ta-mus (quick-er and quick-e-ty)*
3. *Sing and clap with note names e.g. DDDDAAAA (preferably showing a sense of pitch with the hands at the same time)*
4. *Finally, play!*

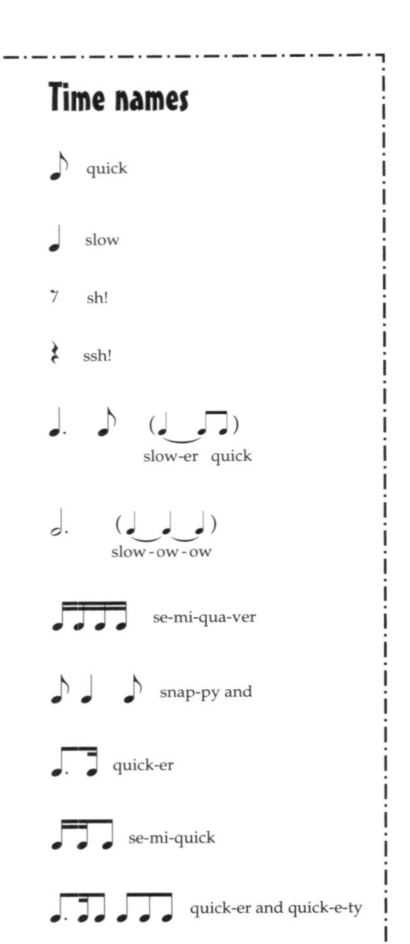

The time names needed in this book are shown to the left.

The windmill symbol is used for circling in the air to loosen up during rests.

The rocket sign is used for pushing the bow arm straight up into the air.

Trace an egg-shape in the air when there is not enough time to do a full windmill.

Versions of **Jackaroo** *for violin and cello are also available, so that pupils can enjoy playing these pieces together. To give the viola and cello a better range, however, you will find that* ***Zebraphants March****,* ***Humming Cat****,* ***Fluttering Butterworm*** *and* ***Waffalo*** *are in different keys from the violin version.*

Finally, encourage children to make these pieces their own by adding second verse words where needed, inventing a new noise on the instrument, or trying out different dynamics. Ask them to create their own imaginary animals to encourage improvisation—they can even draw these into their part!

I hope you have as much fun playing these pieces as Pam and I did in writing them.

Caroline Lumsden

Teaching points

- Security of viola hold
- Freedom of bowing arm

Jackaroo

on an idea by Jim

Suggestion box

1. Sing with the words
2. Sing with note names
3. Play

Teaching point

- Co-ordination of feet and arms

Zebraphants March

on an idea by Olivia

Suggestion box

1. Practise marching
2. Play bars 5–8 from memory
3. Play bars 9–12 from memory

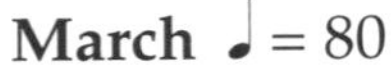

Teaching points

- Rhythmic awareness
- Syncopation

Crocodillo Snap

on an idea by Harry

Suggestion box

1. *Sing words*
2. *Clap with time names*
3. *Practise the 'snap pizz.'*

Teaching points

- Dotted rhythms
- Up-bow start and bow distribution
- Freedom of hip movement

Lazy Chimliroo

on an idea by Harry

Suggestion box

1 Sway and sing with dynamics
2 Repeat, miming the bowing action
3 Play

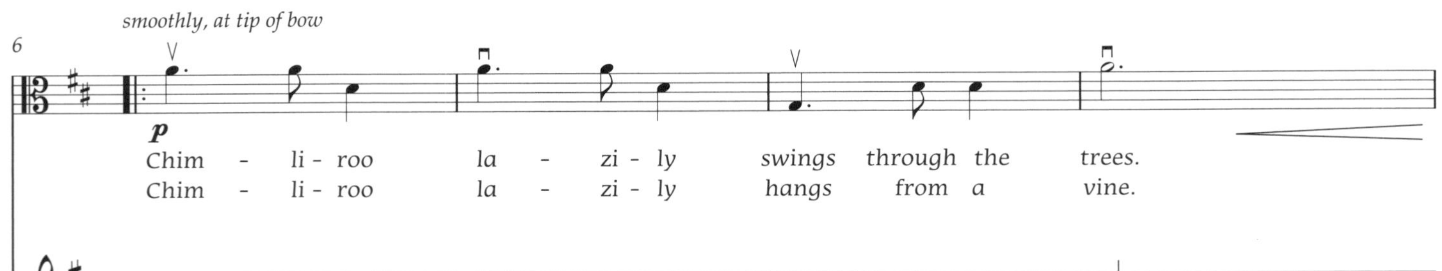

Teaching points

- $\frac{5}{4}$ time signature
- Col legno

on an idea by Katy

Suggestion box

1. Sing words and tap shoulder of viola
2. Play and tap
3. Col legno and tap

Teaching points

- Quality of sound
- Harmonics
- Treble clef†

Suggestion box

1. Hum
2. Learn bars 17–24
3. Learn bars 5–12

† N.B. An easier alternative (without treble clef) is to play bars 17–24 in place of bars 5–12, and to memorize the last four bars.

15
arco
mm
mf
Hum - ming cat fly - ing high, lands in a
mf
20
tree. What a strange crea - ture, he's grin - ning at me.
25
Sing
p
Mm
mm
p
30
arco
pp
Hum - ming cat, hum - ming cat, hum - ming cat sing. Miaow!
pp

Teaching points

- Flexible wrist
- Rotation across strings
- Control of the upper and lower half of the bow

Fluttering Butterworm

on an idea by Phoebe

Suggestion box

1. Holding a pencil, say words whilst moving wrist up and down
2. Play

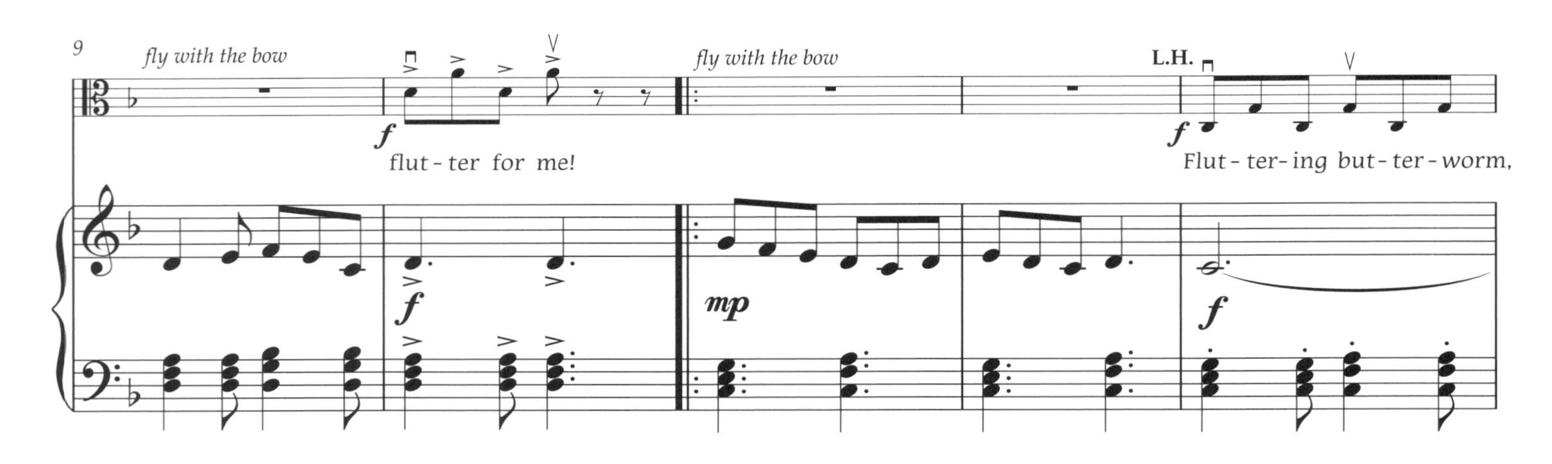

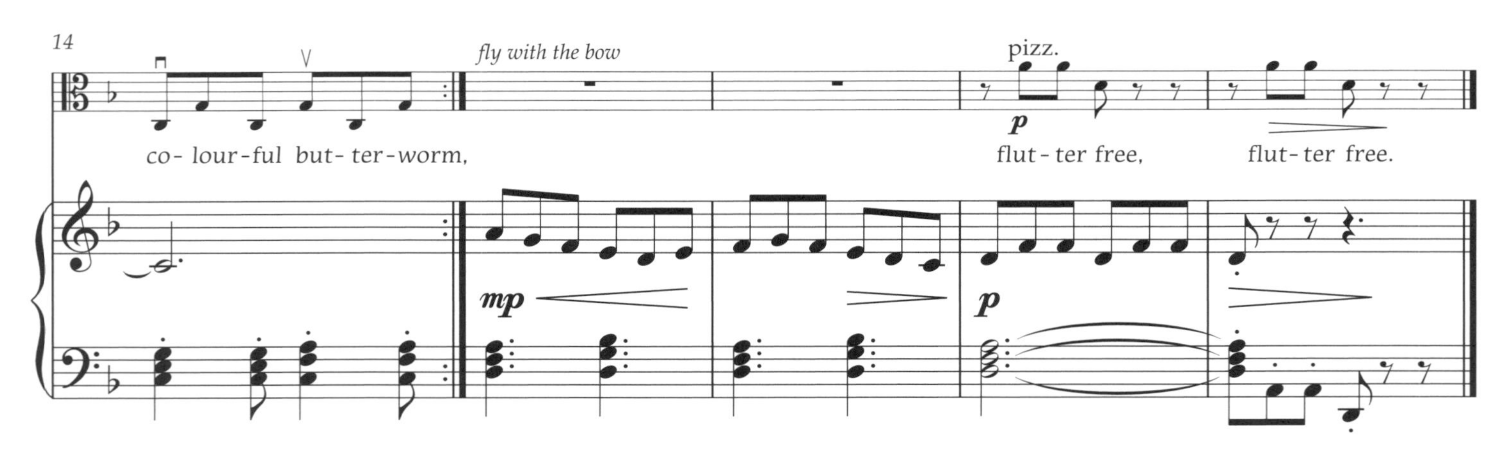

Teaching points

- Bow control
- Glissando

Grunting Boarkey

on an idea by Zoe

Suggestion box

1. Be imaginative with the noises!
2. Learn how to do a glissando
3. Play

Teaching points

- L.H. pizzicato
- Double-stopping

Pythonippotamus

Suggestion box

1. Say and whisper words
2. Play pizzicato bars
3. Play double-stopping bars

Teaching points

- Position of first finger on D and A strings
- Good intonation
- Freedom of bow arm

Jackaroo Jump

Suggestion box

1. Jump on first beat of each bar
2. Practise pizzicato
3. Play

Teaching points

- Staccato bowing
- Position of first finger on G and C strings

Waffalo

on an idea by Sam

Suggestion box

1. Clap
2. Mime, lifting finger up and down in time
3. Play

Teaching points

- Rhythmic control
- Accelerando

Crocodillo Snoring

on an idea by Matthew

Suggestion box

1 Sing with snores and snaps (make arms into crocodile jaw)
2 Play, with snores and snaps

Teaching points

- Co-ordination of bow and finger
- Dynamic awareness

Jungle Footprints

Suggestion box

1 Tiptoe to the beat (stop in rests)
2 Pizz. bars 5–12, then bow
3 Pizz. bars 13–20, then bow

Fluttering Butterworm

on an idea by Phoebe

U.H. = Upper half of the bow
L.H. = Lower half of the bow

With a relaxed wavy movement ♪ = 112

on an idea by Zoe

(circle symbol) = Quick circle with bow (paint an egg-shape in the air)
Glissando = Your teacher will show you how to slide your finger

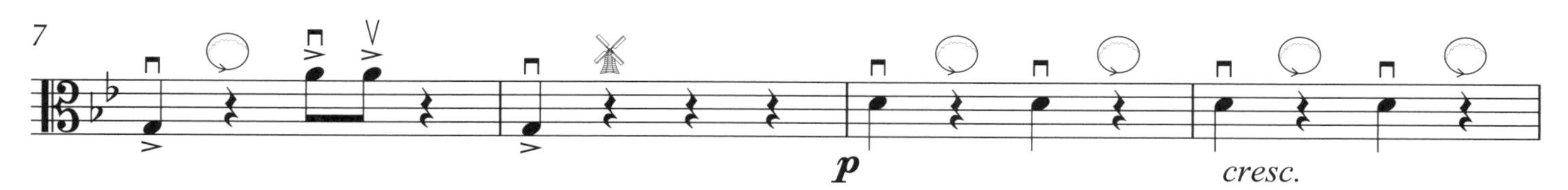

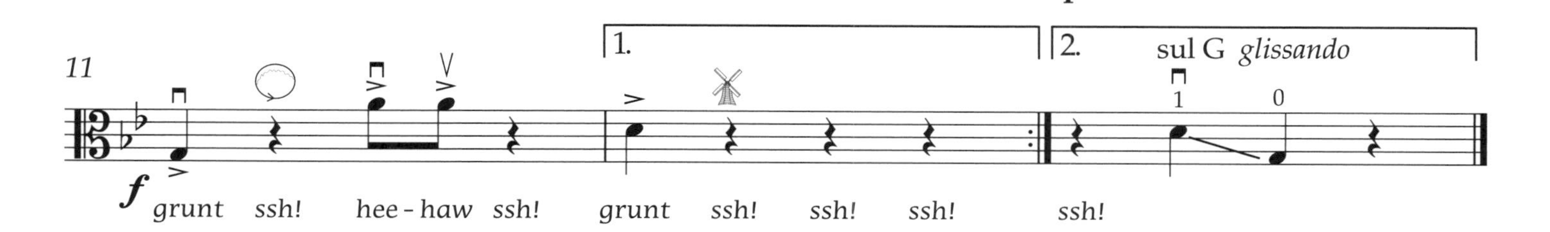

Pythonippotamus

+ = left-hand pizzicato

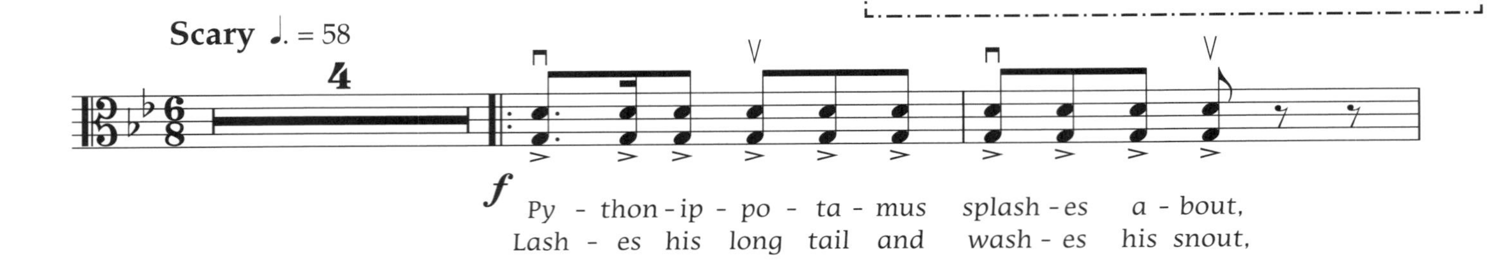

This animal is called a

____

Jackaroo Jump

on an idea by Sam

D.S. 𝄋 al fine = from the sign 𝄋 to the 'fine' (end)

Imaginary Animals

unaccompanied

Now it's your turn to make up your own creatures!

These animals are called: ______________________________

____

____

Crocodillo Snoring

on an idea by Matthew

Yawn with viola = *take both arms up into the air and stretch*

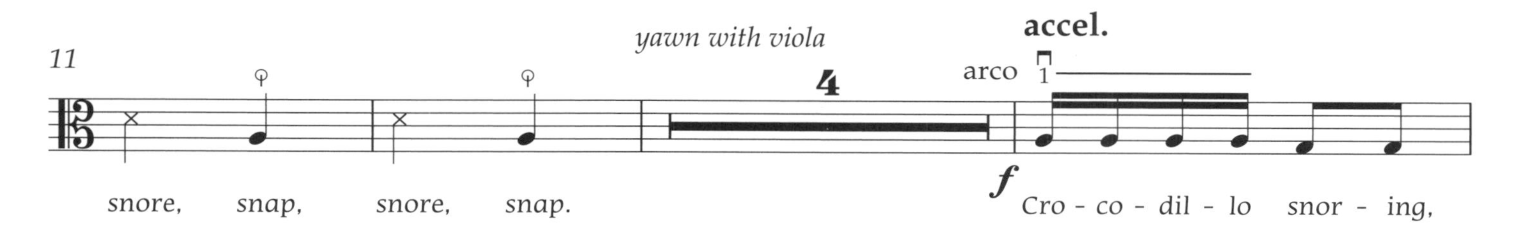

What animal do you think this is?

____

Jungle Footprints

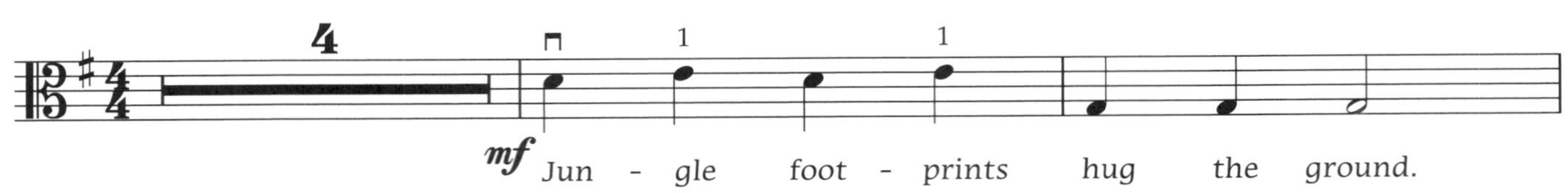

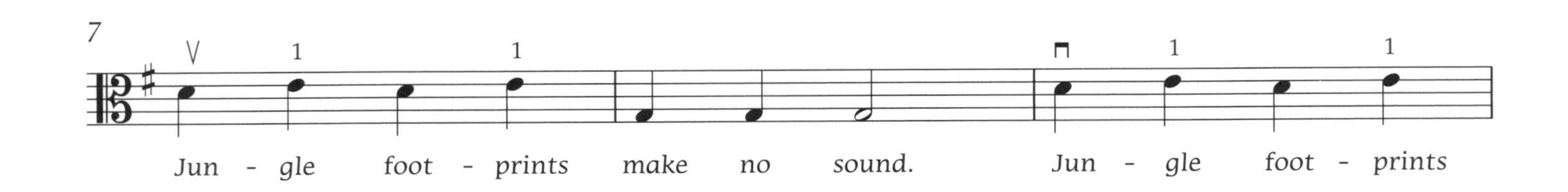

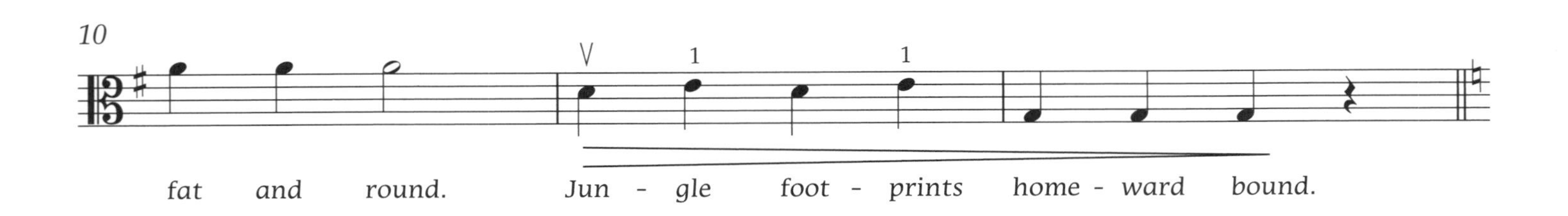

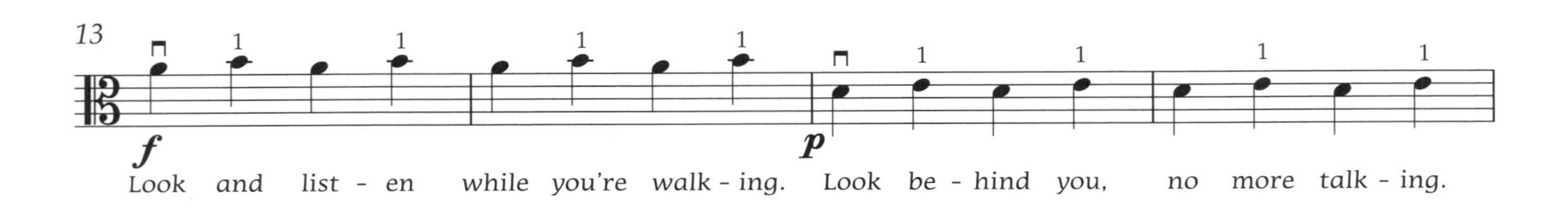

Edition Angewandte

Buchreihe der Universität für angewandte Kunst Wien
Book Series of the University of Applied Arts Vienna

Herausgegeben von / Edited by
Gerald Bast, Rector

edition: 'ʌngewʌndtə

Ernst Logar

Invisible Oil

SpringerWienNewYork

Inhalt

Contents

Ernst Ulrich von Weizsäcker

Vorwort

Erdöl ist eine der wichtigsten Ressourcen: Unser gesamtes Verkehrswesen und damit unser Lebensstil hängen am Öl. Ist das allen bewusst? Scheinbar nein. Wir leben weiter in den Tag hinein, obschon wir uns bedenklich dem „Peak Oil"-Jahr nähern, dem Maximum der globalen Erdölförderung. Die weltweite Nachfrage steigt, weitere, neue große Erdölvorkommen sind nicht absehbar. Treibstoffe aus Ölschiefern oder gar Kohle zu gewinnen ist zwar möglich, aber aus Klimagründen noch weniger verantwortbar. Die Alternative Elektroauto wird kräftig vorangetrieben, aber bislang in der Hauptsache mit Strom aus Kohle und Atomkraft.

Die Öffentlichkeit sieht als wichtigste Alternative die Vermehrung von Sonnen- und Windenergie, und wenn das nicht reicht, Raps-, Mais- und Palmölplantagen. Der Ansatz, Sonne und Wind zu nutzen, ist durchaus eine mögliche Antwort, beide Energieträger stehen aber nicht jederzeit und im gewünschten Ausmaß zur Verfügung; die Biomasseplantagen wiederum sind ökologisch sehr bedenklich, um nicht zu sagen ein Albtraum. Was jedoch in der Diskussion zu kurz kommt, sind die Effizienzsteigerung und eine Zivilisation der Genügsamkeit: Dadurch könnte viel mehr eingespart und damit erreicht werden, als man gemeinhin denkt. Aber für die heutige, von Bildsymbolen strotzende Welt sind Effizienz und Sparsamkeit – im Vergleich zu gleißenden Solarpaneelen und rotierenden Windrädern – schwer vermittelbar. Denn wie soll man das eingesparte Fass Öl oder die nicht erzeugte Kilowattstunde photographieren?

Vielleicht kann die Kunst uns ein Stück weiterhelfen. Sie muss ja nicht die Effizienz illustrieren, aber sie kann das Öl und unsere Abhängigkeit von ihm in den Blick rücken. Genau das tut Ernst Logar. Mit *Invisible Oil* wirft er einen genauen Blick auf uns und auf unsere vom Erdöl dominierte Gesellschaft. Im Zuge seiner Arbeit setzt sich der Künstler intensiv mit diesem Rohstoff auseinander und schafft Werke, die unser Verhältnis und unsere Öl-Sucht reflektieren. Verborgene Zusammenhänge werden eindringlich aufgezeigt. Wer sich auf diese künstlerische Auseinandersetzung mit dem Öl und unserer Sucht danach einlässt, den kann die Schönfärberei derer nicht mehr blenden, die mit dem Verdrängen der weltweiten Notlage Geschäfte machen.

Foreword

Oil is one of the world's most important resources: our entire transport system – and hence our lifestyle – is dependent upon oil and petroleum-related products. Are we all aware of this? Apparently not. We continue on day after day living as we have, although we are rapidly approaching the year of 'Peak Oil'– that year during which the world will extract more oil than it ever has or ever will again. Worldwide demand is growing, while the discovery of further, new large oil reservoirs cannot be expected. While it is possible to extract liquid fuels from oil shale or even coal, that would be even more irresponsible with respect to the Earth's climate. And while the electric car is being promoted heavily as an alternative, such vehicles still have to be powered with electricity produced from coal and nuclear energy.

The public views increased solar and wind energy production as the most important alternative – and if that is not enough, there are also rapeseed, corn and palm oil plantations. While using the sun and the wind certainly is one possible answer, neither energy source is available to us at all times and in the desired amount; biomass plantations, on the other hand, are more than questionable from an ecological standpoint – in fact, they are a nightmare. What receives far too little attention in this discussion is the theme of increasing efficiency and striving to build a civilisation of content frugality: this could help both to conserve and to achieve much more than is commonly believed. But for the present-day world, permeated as it is with visual symbols, the themes of efficiency and frugality are far more difficult to communicate than images of glistening solar panels and rotating wind turbine blades. How, after all, is one to photograph the barrel of oil that did not need to be pumped, the kilowatt hour that went unproduced?

Perhaps art can do something to help us along here. It may not be able to – or even need to – illustrate efficiency as such, but it can indeed shed some light on oil and our oil dependency. Ernst Logar does precisely this. In *Invisible Oil*, he trains his penetrating gaze on us and our petroleum-dominated society. In working on this project, the artist dealt intensely with this natural resource and created works which reflect upon our relationship therewith and addiction thereto. The result is a telling revelation of hidden connections. Those who open their minds to this artistic examination of oil and our oil addiction will no longer be fooled by the spin coming from those who seek to profit from the denial of this worldwide emergency.

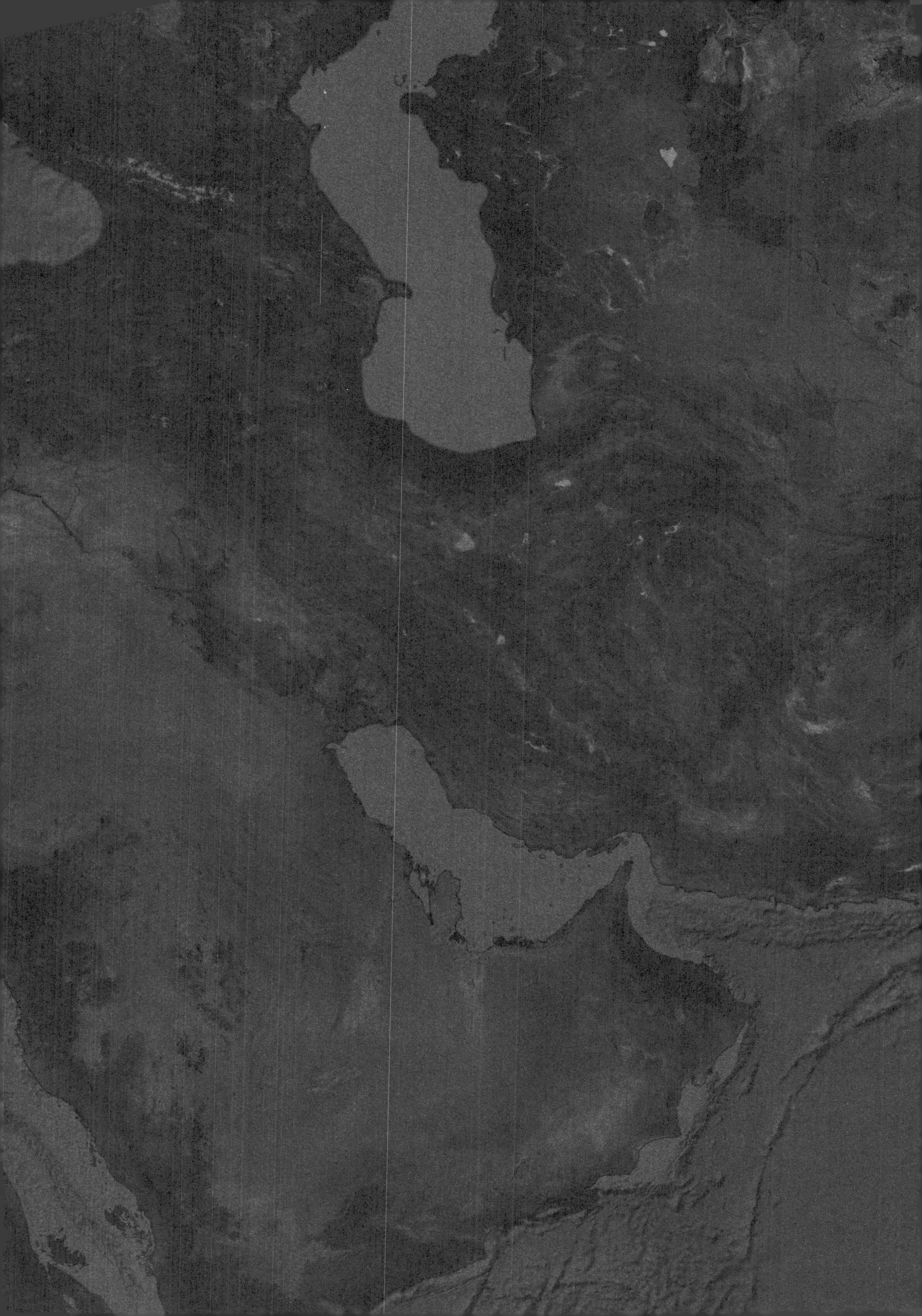

Karin Kneissl

Im Namen des Erdöls

Will man die internationalen Beziehungen der letzten 100 Jahre besser verstehen, so hilft ein Blick auf die Bedeutung des Erdöls bei der Analyse. Mit der Relevanz der Mobilität für die Kriegsführung im Ersten Weltkrieg wurde klar, dass Erdöl zum strategischen Rohstoff aufsteigen sollte. Der britische Politiker Winston Churchill hatte dies rasch begriffen und stellte die englische Flotte von Kohle auf Diesel um. Die deutschen Feldzüge gegen die Sowjetunion und in Nordafrika in den 1940er-Jahren waren von dem Streben Adolf Hitlers getragen, Zugriff auf die Erdölfelder in der Schwarzmeer-Region und im Kaspischen Raum zu erlangen. Auch der französische Premier Georges Clemenceau revidierte nach 1918 seine zuvor noch getätigte Aussage: „Benötige ich Benzin, kaufe ich es bei meinem Apotheker". Denn es wurde für Sieger und Verlierer der großen Kriege des 20. Jahrhunderts gleichermaßen klar, dass es um die physische Kontrolle, den militärisch abgesicherten Zugang zu den Erdölfeldern geht. Dies gilt für unsere Zeit bedauerlicherweise in noch viel größerem Umfang. Krieg und Frieden im Namen des Erdöls prägen die Geschichte des 20. und des noch jungen 21. Jahrhunderts. Im Fall des Irakkriegs sollten alle jene Gegner Recht behalten, auf deren Transparenten während der großen Demonstrationen im Februar 2003 zu lesen war: „no blood for oil".

In the Name of Oil

Anyone who wishes to gain a better understanding of international relations over the past century would do well to consider the significance of oil. The important role played by mobility in the First World War made it clear that oil was on its way to becoming a strategically important national resource. The British politician Winston Churchill was quick to grasp this fact, for which reason he had the British naval fleet converted from coal to diesel power. The 1940s German military campaigns against the Soviet Union and in North Africa were motivated by Adolf Hitler's desire to gain access to the oil fields in the Black Sea and Caspian regions. Similarly, following the year 1918, French Prime Minister Georges Clemenceau was quick to retract his earlier statement that 'when I need petrol, I buy it from my chemist'. For it was equally clear to the winners and the losers of the great 20th-century wars that the main factor was physical control of – and/or militarily ensured access to – oil fields. In our own times, this has unfortunately become even more crucial. War and peace in the name of oil permeate the history of both the 20th and the still-young 21st centuries. With respect to the Iraq war, history has already vindicated those opponents who mounted large-scale demonstrations in 2003 under banners reading: 'no blood for oil'.

Deckten die erdölreichen USA noch 1945 fast 90 Prozent des Treibstoffverbrauchs der Alliierten, entschloss sich Washington in der Folge, die eigenen Vorräte dieses nicht erneuerbaren Energieträgers zu schonen und auf das Erdöl der Arabischen Halbinsel und des Persischen Golfs zu setzen. Das sogenannte Kohlenwasserstoff-Zeitalter hatte begonnen. Das Wirtschaftswunder und die rasche Wohlstandsvermehrung in der nordwestlichen Hemisphäre wären ohne das relativ billige arabische Öl nicht möglich gewesen. Eine der Folgen der neuen und erschwinglichen Mobilität war die Ausdehnung von „Suburbia". Wohnen im Grünen und tägliches Pendeln wurden zum Ideal und Tagestrott. Das bittere Erwachen folgte im Herbst 1973, als sich der Erdölpreis binnen weniger Wochen vervierfachte. Auslöser war ein geopolitisches Ereignis, wie es dann in der Folge noch mehrfach der Fall sein sollte. Der Oktoberkrieg zwischen Israel und einigen seiner arabischen Nachbarstaaten provozierte das Eingreifen der USA zugunsten Israels. Die arabischen Mitglieder der OPEC, der Organisation erdölexportierender Länder, beschlossen ein Erdöl-Embargo für einige Staaten, was einen Preisschock auslöste. Um sich vom nahöstlichen Öl, sprich dem OPEC-Erdöl zu emanzipieren, wurde die Exploration von Nordsee-Öl gefördert. Angesichts des damals sehr hohen Preisniveaus erschienen die teureren Förderungen von Nordsee-Erdöl kommerziell möglich.

Die fossilen Lager der Nordsee waren schon in den 1960er-Jahren bekannt, doch die systematische und massive Förderung begann in dieser Region erst im Zuge der Erdölkrise von 1973. Denn nun waren die höheren Förderkosten, die auf der eingesetzten Technik, den teuren Plattformen und den höheren Personalkosten fußen, infolge des teuren Weltmarktpreises für Erdöl finanzierbar. Die Preisspirale begann sich 1979 infolge der Revolution im Iran neuerlich nach oben zu drehen. Ab Mitte der 1980er-Jahre erlebten wir aber einen Preiseinbruch. Infolge der Rezession in den USA und in Westeuropa und vor allem aufgrund eines Überangebots an Erdöl begann der Preis wieder zu sinken. Heute sind wir mit ähnlichen Schwankungen vor der Kulisse einer noch viel explosiveren weltwirtschaftlichen Lage konfrontiert. Damit wächst wieder das Risiko von Revolten in jenen Ölstaaten, die mangels Einnahmen aus dem Rohstoffexport ihre innere

While the oil-rich United States still covered nearly 90 percent of the Allied demand for fuel in 1945, Washington soon decided to spare its own supplies of this non-renewable resource and instead tap the oil reservoirs of the Arabian Peninsula and the Persian Gulf. The so-called 'hydrocarbon age' had begun. The widespread prosperity that ensued in the North-Western Hemisphere would not have been possible without this relatively cheap Arabian oil. One of the consequences of this new and affordable mobility was the expansion of 'suburbia'. Living in a green environment became the ideal, with the daily commute to work becoming a standard routine. The bitter awakening followed in the autumn of 1973, when the price of oil quadrupled within just a few weeks. The catalyst was a geopolitical event the likes of which were to become common over the next few years. The Yom Kippur War between Israel and several of its Arab neighbours provoked the USA into intervening on Israel's behalf. The Arab members of OPEC, the Organisation of Petroleum-Exporting Countries, decided to respond by imposing an oil embargo on several nations – which resulted in a price shock. In the interest of achieving freedom from Middle Eastern oil – i.e., oil from OPEC producers – a concerted effort then began to develop the oil reserves of the North Sea. The sky-high price level at the time meant that producing the more expensive North Sea oil had become commercially feasible.

The North Sea's fossil fuel reservoirs had been discovered back in the 1960s, but it was not until the oil crisis of 1973 that systematic and massive extraction in the region finally began. It was only then that the high world market price of crude oil could begin to justify the great expense associated with drilling in the North Sea due to the technology required, the costly platforms and the more expensive personnel. With the revolution in Iran in 1979, the oil price once again spiralled upward. From the mid-1980s onward, however, the price collapsed as a consequence of the American and Western European economic recession, as well as – above all – due to a supply glut on the oil market. Today, we are experiencing similar price instability against the backdrop of a far more explosive world economic situation. With this comes an increased risk of revolts in those oil producing states where insufficient

Stabilität nicht sichern können. Vom Kaukasus bis in den Persischen Golf ticken politische Zeitbomben. Sollte es zum Ausfall wichtiger Produzenten kommen, sind Preissprünge wie jene von 1973 nicht auszuschließen. Setzt man also auf das Preisniveau, wenn es um eine Energiewende geht, wird eine solche kaum evolutionär erfolgen. Denn die Volatilität des Erdölpreises führt zu oft unabsehbaren Schwankungen, welche die Budgets von Produzenten und Konsumenten erschüttern.

Rund 450 Bohrinseln machen die Nordsee zum größten Offshore-Fördergebiet. Unter diesen Tiefseebohrungen versteht man die Exploration von Erdöl- und Erdgasfeldern auf dem Meeresboden. Schwierigere geologische und meteorologische Verhältnisse können einen technischen Fehler rasch in einer Katastrophe enden lassen. Die Ölpest im Golf von Mexiko infolge der Explosion auf der BP-Plattform „Deepwater Horizon" im Frühjahr 2010 warf weltweit ein kritisches Schlaglicht auf diese Form der Erdölförderung. Doch der Glaube an die Technik hat Brasilien dazu veranlasst, im Herbst 2010 mit Bohrungen in noch viel größerer Meerestiefe zu starten. Die Herausforderungen an die Ingenieure im Offshore-Bereich sind um ein Vielfaches höher als beispielsweise auf der Arabischen Halbinsel, wo die Produktionskosten pro Fass ein Bruchteil des Aufwands für das Nordsee-Erdöl und -Erdgas sind. Während sich die Reserven im britischen Sektor der Nordsee, mit dem Schwerpunkt in den schottischen Gewässern, ihrem Ende zuneigen, kann sich Norwegen bislang noch als wesentlicher Nicht-OPEC-Produzent behaupten.

Die Peak-Oil-Debatte, die sich um die mögliche Produktionsspitze und den Einbruch des Angebots an Erdöl dreht, spaltet regelmäßig die Gemüter. Während die Anhänger der Peak-Oil-These warnend darauf hinweisen, dass wir möglicherweise bereits die Produktionsspitze überschritten haben und die aktuellen Statistiken für Reserven überhöht seien, wenden die Skeptiker ein: entscheidend sei der Preis. Je höher der Preis für ein Fass Rohöl, umso länger würde die Frist für das letzte Fass hinausgeschoben, zudem sei alles eine Frage der Technologie, die die Exploration verbessere, so die nicht ganz nachvollziehbaren Argumente jener Stimmen, die die Peak-Oil-These ablehnen.

proceeds from crude oil exports make it difficult to ensure domestic security. From the Caucasus to the Persian Gulf, political time bombs are ticking away. If important producers should suddenly be unable to deliver, the possibility of price spikes similar to those of 1973 cannot be excluded. So if change on the energy front is a function of the price level, then such change will hardly take place in an evolutionary fashion. Oil price volatility, after all, often assumes the form of unpredictable swings which wreak havoc on the budgets of both producers and consumers.

Around 450 drilling platforms make the North Sea the world's largest offshore oil region. The terms 'offshore' and 'deep-water' refer to the extraction of oil and natural gas from fields on the ocean floor. Difficult geological and meteorological conditions here mean that a technical malfunction can quickly result in a catastrophe. The spring 2010 oil spill in the Gulf of Mexico following the explosion on the BP platform Deepwater Horizon shed a critical, worldwide spotlight on this form of oil extraction. But even so, unbroken faith in technology moved Brazil to commence drilling in far deeper waters in the autumn of 2010. The engineering challenges involved in offshore drilling are many times greater than, for example, on the Arabian Peninsula, where per-barrel production costs amount to a fraction of what it takes to produce North Sea oil and gas. While the reserves in the British sector of the North Sea (predominantly off the Scottish coast) are rapidly being depleted, Norway is still managing to hold onto its status as a significant non-OPEC producer.

The peak oil debate, which refers to a possible production peak and subsequent drop-off in petroleum product availability, regularly takes on a divisive character. While adherents to the peak oil theory refer warningly that we may have already passed peak production and that current reserve statistics are obsolete, sceptics object: they argue that price is the decisive factor. According to this line of reasoning, the higher the price for a barrel of crude oil goes, the further the date at which the last barrel will be produced gets pushed back; furthermore, they argue, everything is a matter of technology – which will improve exploration. These are the (not entirely logical) arguments of those who reject the peak oil theory.

Unbestritten ist aber, dass es sich bei den fossilen Energieträgern wie Erdöl um endliche Ressourcen handelt, deren Raubbau nicht nur zu Umweltzerstörung, volkswirtschaftlichen Verzerrungen, geopolitischen Problemen et cetera führt, sondern auch einen wesentlichen Rohstoff für andere industrielle Bereiche vernichtet. Es wäre wohl sinnvoller, die 80 Millionen Fass Rohöl, die bislang täglich verbrannt werden, für andere Zwecke einzusetzen oder noch besser aufzusparen. Als der Club of Rome 1972 einen Bericht über die Endlichkeit von Ressourcen veröffentlichte, wurde diese Problematik erstmals thematisiert. Zwar irrten sich die Autoren bei ihren Fristen, doch viel entscheidender ist der Kern der Botschaft, der seither nur an Brisanz gewonnen hat. Die Berechnungen zum ökologischen Fußabdruck zeigen es auf: Wenn wir so weitermachen, bedienen wir uns an den Bodenschätzen der Erde, an den Ackerflächen, am Wasser usw. auf Kredit. In welchem Umfang wir die Erde auf Pump gebrauchen, lässt sich am Datum des sogenannten „World Overshoot Day" ablesen. War dieser 2009 noch am 26. September, wurde er für 2010 bereits mit dem 21. August berechnet. Dies bedeutet, dass die Menschheit in weniger als neun Monaten ihr gesamtes Jahresbudget an Umweltressourcen aufbraucht, wie die Analyse von Greenpeace und World Wildlife Fund zeigt.

Um auf diese unverrückbaren Tatsachen zu reagieren, setzte sich die Europäische Union im März 2007 hohe Ziele. Die Strategie „20-20-20", die u. a. eine Reduzierung der CO_2-Emissionen um 20 Prozent bis 2020 vorsieht, hat aber große Mängel. Je heftiger die Wirtschaftskrise ausfällt, desto schwieriger wird die Umsetzung dieser Energiepolitik, die sich als Solidaritätsvertrag zwischen den Generationen versteht. Logischer erschiene, eine nachhaltige Energiepolitik allein deswegen zu verfolgen, weil klimatische Veränderungen zu Naturkatastrophen und auch Kriegen führen. Wenn Hochwasser in Europa und nicht nur in Bangladesch wüten, rufen deren Schäden die Versicherungen auf den Plan. Vor allem die großen Rückversicherer kooperieren mit Umweltschutzorganisationen bei der Förderung von Investitionen in CO_2-arme Projekte. Wenn New York unter Wasser steht, kommen nachhaltige Gegenmaß-

Beyond dispute, however, is that fossil energy sources such as oil are finite resources whose reckless exploitation leads not only to environmental destruction, economic distortions, geopolitical problems, etc., but also implies the destruction of important resources which are vital to other industrial areas. It would probably make more sense to use the 80 million barrels of crude oil which we have so far been burning every day for other purposes – or better still, to conserve them. When the Club of Rome released its widely noted report on the finite nature of natural resources back in 1972, it was the first time that this problem had been placed front and centre. While its authors' projections may have been wrong in terms of timing, this has no bearing on the importance of their basic message – the relevance of which has since grown more and more urgent. Calculations of our ecological footprint confirm this: if we keep on as we have so far, we will be continuing to use the Earth's mineral resources, agricultural land, water, etc. on credit. The extent to which we are overdrawing our stock of available resources can be seen every year in terms of the date known as 'World Overshoot Day'. While we reached this point on 26 September in 2009, the 2010 day was calculated to have occurred as early as 21 August. In other words, according to the analysis by Greenpeace and the World Wildlife Fund, humankind used up its entire 2010 resource budget in less than nine months.

In response to such indisputable facts, March 2007 saw the European Union set itself some challenging goals. But its so-called '20-20-20' strategy, which entails a 20-percent reduction of CO_2 emissions by 2020, is fraught with problematic elements. The more severe the economic crisis turns out to be, the more difficult it will become to implement this EU energy policy, which is touted as a gesture of solidarity between the generations. It would seem far more logical to pursue a sustainable energy policy for the simple reason that climatic changes lead to natural disasters and war. When floods rage in Europe and not just in Bangladesh, the resulting damage has serious effects on insurance companies. The larger reinsurers have therefore begun cooperating with environmental protection organisations to sponsor investments in low-carbon projects. After all, when New York is underwater, it will be too

nahmen zu spät. Finanzmärkte arbeiten unter kurzen Zeithorizonten, wobei ein Quartal fast langfristig anmutet. Das Klima verändert sich leise und in langen Perioden. Um das vage Konzept der Nachhaltigkeit mit Substanz zu füllen, wäre es an der Zeit, dem Thema Energie institutionell gerecht zu werden. Der Vorwurf an die EU, keine Energiepolitik zu haben, gründet sich auf viele Ursachen. Eine davon liegt im Fehlen nationaler Hierarchien. Energiepolitik wird interministeriell gebastelt, anstatt Energieministerien diese strategische Materie zu übertragen und der Europäischen Kommission mehr Kompetenzen zu gewähren.

Das Thema Erdöl und Energiepolitik ist voller unterschiedlicher Dimensionen, die von der Sicherheitspolitik, vom Umweltschutz über Urbanismus bis hin zum alten Zwist zwischen Brüssel und den Nationalstaaten betreffend Übertragung von Zuständigkeiten reichen. Betrachtet der „Wall Street Refiner" den Ölmarkt exklusiv über seinen Bildschirm und seine Preischarts, konzentriert sich der Analyst für Sicherheitspolitik auf die militärischen Allianzen, die zwecks Sicherung der Energieversorgung zu pflegen sind. Ernst Logar unternimmt mit seinem Ansatz als Künstler eine sehr vielschichtige Annäherung, indem er sich vom konkreten Schicksal der Stadt Aberdeen, von ihren Menschen und ihrer Stadtplanung inspirieren und berühren ließ und das oft unsichtbare Wirken des Erdöls sichtbar macht.

Dass Ölkonzerne sich in den letzten Jahren allmählich in Energiekonzerne verwandelt haben, die wie BP mit dem Logo der Sonnenblume und als Kämpfer für Nachhaltigkeit auftreten, war nur beschränkt erfolgreich. Mehr Mittel werden in die Vermarktung dieses neuen Image gesteckt als in die Grundlagenforschung. Noch geht es um „Big Oil & Big Money". Die Umwandlung des nationalen oder gar globalen Energiemix wird sich wohl mangels politischen Willens und finanzieller Bereitschaft noch hinziehen.

late to implement long-term preventive measures. Financial markets work with a view to the short term, in which the time until the next quarter seems like a near-eternity. The climate, on the other hand, changes quietly and over truly long phases. In order to lend substance to the vague concept of sustainability, it is high time we began doing justice to our energy predicament on an institutional level. There are many reasons for which one could accuse the EU of not actually having an energy policy, one of which is the absence of quasi-national policymaking structures. In Europe, energy policy is formulated between each member-state's numerous ministries, rather than dedicated energy ministries being created to handle this strategically crucial material and more competencies being assigned to the European Commission.

The topic of oil and energy policy has numerous and diverse dimensions, ranging from security policy and environmental protection to urbanism and right on to the old conflict between Brussels and the EU member states over the transfer of responsibilities and authority. While "Wall Street refiners" regard the oil market exclusively in terms of the price charts on their computer screens, security analysts focus on the military alliances that must be tended to in the interest of ensuring a continuous energy supply. Ernst Logar, on the other hand, uses his artistic approach to generate a highly multilayered analysis: Logar allows himself to be inspired and touched by the concrete fate of the city of Aberdeen, its citizens and its urban planning, and the resulting works reveal oil's widespread and often invisible effects.

Recent efforts by the oil conglomerates to gradually transform themselves into energy conglomerates, as expressed by BP's sunflower logo and sustainability slogans, have met with only limited success. More capital has gone into the marketing of this new image than into actual basic research. It continues to be all about 'big oil and big money'. The transformation of national energy mixes, to say nothing of the global energy mix, will therefore likely be slow in coming – due to a lack of will and wherewithal that is both political and economic in nature.

Northfield, Aberdeen

Peter Troxler

Die Hauptstadt des Erdöls

Aberdeen durchlief in den 1960er-Jahren eine wirtschaftliche Depression; die vorherrschenden Industrien der Fischverarbeitung, des Schiffbaus und der Textilindustrie waren bereits im Niedergang begriffen. Doch schon damals – und das ist wichtig, um die soziale und ökonomische Struktur von Aberdeen zu verstehen – galt Aberdeen als bedeutendes regionales Dienstleistungszentrum. 55 Prozent der Beschäftigten waren im Dienstleistungssektor tätig.

Die Entdeckung des Nordseeöls in den späten Sechzigern und der darauf folgende Umzug der Ölindustrie nach Aberdeen kamen für die lokale Wirtschaft gerade recht. Sie brachten Arbeitsplätze und stoppten somit Abwanderung und Arbeitslosigkeit; national gesehen kompensierte dies zumindest teilweise die gedrosselte Produktion der OPEC-Länder zu Beginn der 1970er-Jahre.

Im scharfen Gegensatz zu den traditionellen Industrien im Nordosten Schottlands war die Ölindustrie dem internationalen Wettbewerb ausgesetzt und nicht Gegenstand des Protektionismus staatlicher Regulation durch die Labour- und konservativen Regierungen. Damals gab es „dringendere Probleme für diese Regierungen, als infrage zu stellen, was eine sehr ertragreiche Steuerquelle zu sein schien“ (Harris u.a. 1988, S. 31).

Oil and the City

In the 1960s, Aberdeen's economy was relatively depressed, with the fish processing, shipbuilding and textiles industries all very much already in decline. If one is to understand the city's social and economic structure, it is important to remember that even then Aberdeen was a significant regional service centre, accounting for 55 per cent of employment in the service sector.

The discovery of North Sea oil in the late 60s and the subsequent relocation of the oil industry to Aberdeen was more than timely. In a local context, it counteracted emigration and impending unemployment in Aberdeen, and in the national context it compensated, at least in part, for falling oil supply after OPEC's cuts in the early 70s.

In sharp contrast to the traditional industries in the North East of Scotland, the oil industry was dominated by international competition rather than by national protection and regulation from Labour and Conservative governments. And at the time there were 'more pressing problems for these governments than to challenge what appeared to be a very successful tax revenue system' (Harris et al. 1988, p. 31).

Hafen, Aberdeen | Aberdeen Harbour

Hafen, Aberdeen | Aberdeen Harbour

Es war wohl dieser Steuersegen, der die britische Regierung jahrelang gegenüber dem Sinken der nationalen Produktivität im internationalen Vergleich blind machte. Er war wohl auch dafür verantwortlich, dass die Stadtverwaltung von Aberdeen die sich ausweitende Kluft zwischen Reichen und Armen, die noch durch die geschlechtsspezifische Selektivität der Ölindustrie verschärft wurde, lange Zeit nicht wahrnahm. Das Aufblühen der Ölindustrie wie vermutlich auch die Geschwindigkeit und Entschlossenheit, mit der das geschah, ihr Bedarf an auswärtigen Arbeitskräften – Nordengland und Zentralschottland sind weit genug weg, um im Nordosten Schottlands als „auswärtig" zu gelten – und die Riesenmenge an Geld, die im Spiel war, haben, so scheint es, Bevölkerung und Regierung gleichermaßen überrumpelt. Die Bevölkerung fürchtete und beklagte die Zunahme an Kriminalität, Prostitution und alkoholbedingter Gewalt. Den Zuständigen in Politik und Verwaltung mangelte es sowohl an strategischem Verständnis, um den Anforderungen dieser neuen Industrie gerecht zu werden, als auch an einem Programm, um die Probleme effizient zu lösen.

It is probably this revenue success that blinded successive UK national governments to the nation's diminishing productivity. It might also have blinded local governments to the increasing inequality between the haves and the have-nots that was accentuated by the gender selectivity of the oil industry. The arrival of the oil industry, and probably also the speed and determination of its growth, its need for foreign labour – north England and central Scotland being far afield enough to count as foreign in the North East – and the sheer amounts of money involved seemed to overwhelm the populace and officials of Aberdeen alike. Ordinary people feared and complained about an increase in crime, prostitution and drink-related violence. Officials lacked a strategic understanding to respond to the requirements of this new industry or tactics to deal effectively with the problems.

Trainingszentrum | Training Centre, Bridge of Don, Aberdeen

King's Links, Aberdeen

21

Eine Auswirkung der sich breitmachenden Ölindustrie auf Aberdeen war, dass bestehende Industrien vertrieben wurden. Entscheidend waren mindestens drei Faktoren: Die Lohnkosten stiegen auf ein für traditionelle Industrien unerschwingliches Niveau, Immobilienpreise kletterten in für Arbeiter in anderen Industrien unbezahlbare Höhen, was zur Suburbanisierung weiter Bereiche des umliegenden Aberdeenshire führte, und um Industrie- und Gewerbezonen entstand ein heftiger Wettbewerb. Aus denselben Gründen kam Aberdeen für andere Industrien als Standort nicht in Frage; die Elektronikindustrie gilt dafür als das bekannteste Beispiel. Eine weitere Auswirkung war möglicherweise die Stärkung des Dienstleistungssektors. Obgleich sich dieser sehr eng auf die Ölfirmen konzentrierte, wurde damit doch der Charakter Aberdeens als Dienstleistungszentrum gestärkt.

Das führte zu einer Überabhängigkeit von einer monolithischen Industrie, die beinahe ausschließlich von multinationalen Unternehmen mit Sitz im Ausland dominiert wird. Diese sind bereit, ihre Niederlassungen international jederzeit dahin umzusiedeln, wo es am geeignetsten erscheint. Die lokale Wirtschaft wurde in beunruhigendem Ausmaß von der Ölindustrie abhängig – heute entfallen auf einen direkt in der Ölindustrie Tätigen nur 1,78 Arbeitsplätze in der lokalen Wirtschaft.

One effect of the coming of oil to Aberdeen was the displacement of existing industries. There were at least three mechanisms: an increase in the cost of labour to a level unaffordable by traditional industries, a rise in house prices to a level out of the reach of workers in other industries, leading to suburbanisation of vast areas in the Shire, and the competition for commercial and industrial property. For the same reasons, other industries did not consider Aberdeen a viable place to move to, the electronics industry being the most oft-cited example. A third effect may have been the strengthening of the service sector. This was very narrowly focused on the oil companies, but nonetheless reinforced the 'service centre' character of Aberdeen.

In consequence, these developments led to overdependence on one monolithic industry, dominated by highly mobile overseas corporations, ready to move elsewhere if and when needed. The local economy developed an unsettling dependence on the oil industry – today an estimated 1.78 jobs are generated in the local economy for every direct employee in the industry itself.

Tillydrone, Aberdeen

Doch zu dieser Zeit war sich noch niemand bewusst, dass „die zunehmende Verwendung des mobilen Verbrennungsmotors eine dramatische – um nicht zu sagen zerstörerische – Veränderung so mancher Alltagsgegebenheiten für Großbritannien, speziell in Städten, mit sich bringen würde" (Button 1976, S. 25) und dass diese Veränderung „bis zum Jahr 2000 die Voraussetzungen für ökonomische und soziale Zusammenbrüche auf katastrophalem Niveau schaffen würde" (ebd., S. 27).

Auch wenn ökonomische und soziale Zusammenbrüche Aberdeen noch nicht in vollem Ausmaß erreicht haben, hat sich die ökonomische Landschaft bereits sichtbar verändert. Im Jahr 2003 bemerkte BBC-Korrespondent James Arnold eine subtile, aber bedeutsame Veränderung in Aberdeen. Die Beschilderung, die Aberdeen an jedem Kreisverkehr als „the oil capital of Europe" (Ölhauptstadt Europas) beworben hatte, war durch „energy capital of Europe" (Energiehauptstadt Europas) ersetzt worden (Arnold 2003).

At that time nobody was aware that the 'increase in the use of the mobile internal combustion engine has wrought a dramatic – some would say devastating – change in many features of everyday life in the UK, especially in cities' (Button 1976, p. 25), and that this change would be 'setting the stage for economic and social disruption on a catastrophic scale by the year 2000' (ibid., p. 27).

Economic and social disruption has not yet arrived in Aberdeen to its full extent, although the economic landscape has already changed considerably. In 2003, the BBC's James Arnold noted a subtle but significant change in Aberdeen. The little signs on the roundabouts that used to brand the city as 'the oil capital of Europe' were now changed to 'energy capital of Europe' (Arnold 2003).

Zentrum, Aberdeen | Aberdeen Centre

Offiziellen Quellen zufolge hat das Nordseeöl sein Fördermaximum vor etwa zehn Jahren, im Jahr 1999, erreicht (DTI 2007, S. 109). Die Kosten für die Entwicklung und Produktion von Öl und Gas in Großbritannien steigen weiterhin. Nach eigenen Untersuchungen kann die Industrie Öl aus einer neuen Quelle erst ab einem Preis von etwa über 40 Dollar pro Fass kostendeckend produzieren. Die Anzahl neu angebohrter Quellen geht konstant zurück: 2009 waren es 65 von 77 geplanten, 2010 waren es 62 von 73 geplanten, für 2011 sind 67 geplant (Oil & Gas UK 2009, Oil & Gas UK 2010). Es ist kein Wunder, dass sich die Ölindustrie nun Hilfe vom Staat zur Behebung der Misere erwartet, in die sie sich selbst hineinmanövriert hat.

Officially, North Sea Oil production peaked some ten years ago, in 1999 (DTI 2007, p. 109). The cost of developing and producing UK oil and gas is rising. According to the industry's own activity survey, the breakeven price of oil for a new well is just over $40 a barrel. The number of new wells being drilled annually has been both decreasing and consistently below projections: 2009 saw 65 of 77 planned wells actually drilled, in 2010 it was 62 of 73, and the drilling of only 67 new wells is projected for 2011 (Oil & Gas UK 2009, Oil & Gas UK 2010). The industry, unsurprisingly, is looking to the government for assistance and to solve the miserable situation they have let themselves slip into.

Zentrum, Aberdeen | Aberdeen Centre

Gesamtwirtschaftlich gesehen sind die Immobilienverkäufe im letzten Quartal des Jahres 2008 auf beinahe die Hälfte des Vorjahres, von 1.662 auf 894, eingebrochen. Dies ist zugleich das erste Mal seit den frühen 1990ern, dass sie unter 1.000 pro Quartal fielen (Crighton 2009). Im Jahr 2009 kam es zu einer leichten Erholung, während 2010 einen erneuten Rückgang brachte, auch wenn dieser nicht so stark war wie im Jahr 2008 (Crighton 2011). Noch 2007 hatte die öffentlich-private Partnerschaftsorganisation Aberdeen City and Shire Economic Future (ACSEF) ein Manifest zum wirtschaftlichen Wachstum entwickelt, das Aberdeen vorhersagte, „im Jahr 2025 [...] einer der robustesten und widerstandsfähigsten Wirtschaftsräume in Europa zu sein – mit dem Ruf, neue Möglichkeiten für Unternehmertum und Erfindergeist zu bieten, die Weltklassetalente aller Altersgruppen anziehen und [an Aberdeen] binden werden" (ACSEF 2007). Gleichzeitig brachte sich die Stadt Aberdeen mit Ausgaben, die drei Jahre lang das Budget überschritten, in eine „prekäre finanzielle Lage", wie ein externer Rechnungsprüfer feststellte (Audit Scotland (a) 2008). Aberdeen muss massiv sparen, doch die eingesetzte Rechnungsprüfungskommission ist nicht „zuversichtlich, dass diese Einsparungen erreicht werden" (Audit Scotland (b) 2008).

Die Beschäftigten in Aberdeen gehören noch immer zu den besser bezahlten – der mittlere Bruttowochenverdienst beträgt £ 481 im Vergleich zum schottischen Mittel von £ 432. Die Arbeitslosigkeit

In the economy at large, the last quarter of 2008 has seen a collapse in house sales in Aberdeen to almost half of what they were a year before, from 1,662 to 894. This is the first time since the early 90s that they have dropped below 1,000 in any quarter (Crighton 2009). Sales were slow to recover in 2009, and in 2010 the housing market collapsed anew – albeit less severely than in 2008 (Crighton 2011). While 2007 saw the public private partnership Aberdeen City and Shire Economic Future (ACSEF) develop its manifesto for economic growth, projecting Aberdeen 'by 2025 [...] to be recognised as one of the most robust and resilient economies in Europe with a reputation for opportunity, enterprise and inventiveness that will attract and retain world-class talent of all ages' (ACSEF 2007). Aberdeen City Council itself was in a 'precarious financial position', as its external auditor found, with expenditure in excess of its budget over a three year period (Audit Scotland (a) 2008). Aberdeen is in need of substantial savings, but the audit commission does not have 'confidence that these savings will be delivered' (Audit Scotland (b) 2008).

Aberdeen's working population is still relatively affluent – gross average weekly earnings are £ 481 compared to a Scottish average of £ 432, unemployment is 1.5 percent compared to the 3.2 percent Scottish average. Yet the city has seen an increase in the number of neighbourhoods

St. Fergus Gas Terminal

Tillydrone, Aberdeen

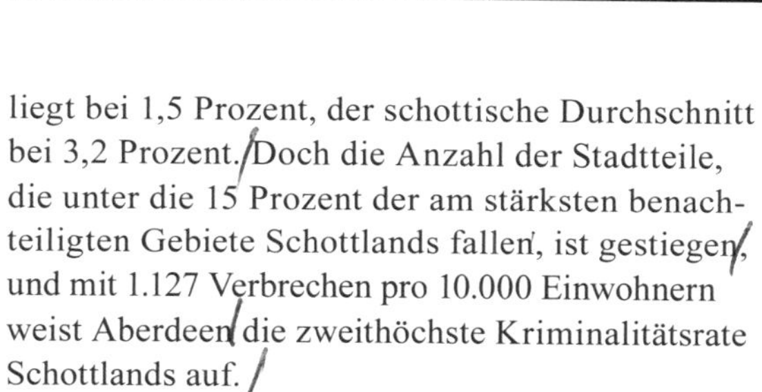

liegt bei 1,5 Prozent, der schottische Durchschnitt bei 3,2 Prozent. Doch die Anzahl der Stadtteile, die unter die 15 Prozent der am stärksten benachteiligten Gebiete Schottlands fallen, ist gestiegen, und mit 1.127 Verbrechen pro 10.000 Einwohnern weist Aberdeen die zweithöchste Kriminalitätsrate Schottlands auf.

Wenn es um das Thema Zukunftspläne und Nachhaltigkeit geht, ist Aberdeen zwar die erste Stadt in Schottland, die beim European Covenant of Mayors mitmachen will, der sich das Ziel gesetzt hat, Kohlendioxidemissionen bis 2020 über das EU-Ziel von 20 Prozent hinaus zu reduzieren. Doch 478 andere europäische Städte haben sich der Initiative bereits früher angeschlossen. Die heutigen Stadtentwicklungspläne scheinen den Ehrgeiz Aberdeens kaum zu unterstützen: Das prognostizierte Bevölkerungswachstum um etwa 40.000 Bewohner bis 2030 wird die Zersiedelung rund um die Stadt unweigerlich verschärfen: 51.000 neue Gebäude sollen auf bisher ungenutzten Flächen und im benachbarten Aberdeenshire entstehen, nur 15.000 in bestehenden Bauzonen oder Umwidmungszonen. Nachhaltigkeit bedeutete in den vergangenen zehn Jahren für das offizielle Aberdeen, „ökonomischen Wohlstand zu sichern [...], Ungleichheiten zu beseitigen und Chancen für breitere Schichten zu schaffen, gestützt auf eine Partnerschaft, die alle Sektoren der Gesellschaft einschließt" (Aberdeen City Council 1998) – eine Beschreibung mit auffallend schwach ausgeprägtem Umweltaspekt.

dropping into 'the most deprived 15 percent of Scottish data-zones' – and at 1,127 recorded crimes per 10,000 population the crime rate is the second highest in Scotland.

When it comes to future plans and sustainability, Aberdeen might be the first city in Scotland to sign up to the European Covenant of Mayors, which aims to reduce carbon dioxide emissions beyond the EU target of 20 % by 2020, but 478 other European cities joined the initiative earlier. And current structural plans hardly seem to support this ambition: a projected population growth in the North East of some 40,000 by 2030 is poised to increase city sprawl, with 51,000 new buildings planned on greenfield sites and in the neighbouring Shire villages, compared to only 15,000 on brownfield and regeneration sites in the city. Sustainability, for the last ten years in official Aberdeen, meant 'to seek to ensure economic prosperity [...], tackle inequalities and widen opportunity and be based on a partnership involving all sectors of the community' (Aberdeen City Council 1998), carrying an obviously weak environmental emphasis.

Konferenzraum | Conference room, Oil & Gas UK, Aberdeen

Unsichtbar hat das Öl einen Lebensstil sowie urbane und soziale Strukturen geschaffen, die von der allgegenwärtigen Verfügbarkeit des schwarzen Goldes abhängen. Produktion und Raffination von Öl bringen Arbeitsplätze und Rendite auf investiertes Kapital. Als leicht zu transportierende Energiequelle verstärkt es lokale und globale Transportströme. Als weitverbreiteter Grundbestandteil vieler unserer täglichen Produkte ist es die Ressource Nummer eins der Kohlenstoffgesellschaft. Dies ist keinesfalls auf Aberdeen beschränkt, doch macht der Genius Loci die Sache kaum anderswo sichtbarer. In Zeiten finanzieller und ökologischer Krisen, für die das unbarmherzige Streben nach ökonomischem Wachstum eine der Hauptursachen ist (Jackson 2009, S. 12), scheint es verführerisch, die Machthabenden zu beschuldigen und ihnen die Pflicht aufzuerlegen, eine Lösung zu finden. Das Anpangern ihrer Heimlichtuerei und ihrer wohlgehüteten Geschäftsgeheimnisse mag wohl dazu beitragen, dass sie diese Aufgabe auch ernst nehmen. Doch Unsichtbares sichtbar machen, bringt auch Unangenehmes ans Licht – denn wir alle sind, in größerem oder geringerem Ausmaß, Komplizen, was das Verbrechen kohlenstoffbasierter Annehmlichkeiten angeht. Um die Welt einmal verändern zu können, müssen wir unseren eigenen Lebenstil, unsere Ambitionen und Träume prüfen, hinterfragen und verändern.

Invisibly, oil has created lifestyles and urban and societal structures that are dependent on the ubiquitous availability of the black gold. The extraction and refinement of oil provide jobs and revenue on capital invested. As an easily portable source of energy it fuels local and worldwide transport. Its widespread use as an ingredient in many of our daily products makes it the number one resource of the carbon economy. This is not limited to Aberdeen; yet hardly anywhere else is the genius loci more prominently promoting the cause. In times when the world faces financial and ecological crises, of which the relentless pursuit of economic growth is a root cause (Jackson 2009, p. 12), one could be inclined to look to those in power to accept responsibility and the burden of finding a solution. Unveiling their hidden practices, their well-kept operational secrets might contribute to them accepting their role. Yet uncovering the invisible is bound to reveal the more uncomfortable – that to a greater or lesser extent, everybody is complicit in committing the carbon commodity crime. To eventually change the world it is our own lifestyle, ambitions and dreams that we have to check, question and amend.

Büro | Office RMT-OILC, Aberdeen

Bibliografie | Bibliography

Aberdeen City Council. Aberdeen City Local Plan Consultative Draft. 1998.

ACSEF. Building on Energy. The Economic Manifesto for Aberdeen City and the Shire. 2007. http://www.acsef.co.uk/infoPage.cfm?pageID=2 (Stand: 5.4.2009/accessed 5 April 2009).

Arnold, James. A burst of energy in Europe's oil capital. 12.11.2003. http://news.bbc.co.uk/2/hi/business/3236703.stm (Stand: 5.4.2009/accessed 5 April 2009).

Audit Scotland (a). Aberdeen City Council: Annual Audit 2007/08. A report by the Controller of Audit to the Accounts Commission under Section 102(1) of the Local Government (Scotland) Act 1973 (SR/2009/1). 2008. http://www.audit-scotland.gov.uk/utilities/search_report.php?id=1006 (Stand: 5.4.2009/accessed 5 April 2009).

Audit Scotland (b). Aberdeen City Council. The Audit of Best Value and Community Planning. 2008. http://www.audit-scotland.gov.uk/docs/local/2008/bv_080529_aberdeen_city.pdf (Stand: 5.4.2009/accessed 5 April 2009).

Button, John (Hg./ed.). The Shetland Way of Oil. Reactions of a Small Community to Big Business. Thuleprint, Sandwick 1976.

Crighton, Ryan. Dreadful Property Slump May Get Worse – Warning. North-east house sales dire, says ASPC chief. Aberdeen Press & Journal, 13.2.2009. http://www.pressandjournal.co.uk/Article.aspx/1062778 (Stand: 5.4.2009/accessed 5 April 2009).

Crighton, Ryan. Big slump in Scottish property sales. Aberdeen Press & Journal, 2.2.2011. http://www.pressandjournal.co.uk/Article.aspx/2117331 (Stand: 7.3.2011/accessed 7 March 2011).

DTI. Meeting the Energy Challenge, Department of Trade and Industry. Cm 7124, London 2007. http://www.official-documents.gov.uk/document/cm71/7124/7124.asp (Stand: 5.4.2009/accessed 5 April 2009).

Harris, Anthony, Lloyd H., Gregory M., Newlands, David A. The Impact of Oil on the Aberdeen Economy. Aldershot, Avebury 1988.

Jackson, Tim. Prosperity without Growth? – The transition to a sustainable economy. Sustainable Development Commission, 2009. http://www.sd-commission.org.uk/publications.php?id=914 (Stand: 5.4.2009/accessed 5 April 2009).

Oil & Gas UK. 2008 Activity Survey. 2009. http://www.oilandgas.org.uk/issues/economic/econ08/index.cfm (Stand: 5.4.2009/accessed 5 April 2009).

Oil & Gas UK. 2011 Activity Survey. 2011. http://www.oilandgasuk.co.uk/templates/asset-relay.cfm?frmAssetFileID=1257 (Stand: 7.3.2011/accessed 7 March 2011).

Fire alarm
NO PARKING
24 HOUR
ACCESS
REQUIRED
CCTV
in operation

Pipeline | Dyce, Aberdeen

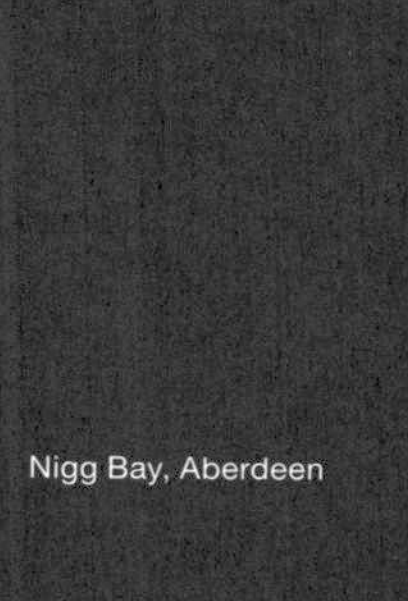

Nigg Bay, Aberdeen

Tillydrone

Logie

Northfield

Woodside

Torry

Ausstellungsansicht 1 | Exhibition view 1

Alejandra Rodríguez-Remedi

Durch einen Spiegel, in einem dunklen Wort: Visualisierung, Enthüllung und Reflexion in Ernst Logars *Invisible Oil*

Das Produkt erfüllt seinen Zweck großteils ungesehen, indem es seinen Weg in Verbrennungsmotoren oder generell auf den Energiemarkt findet. Die Verbindung zu seiner Quelle oder zum Prozess seiner Entwicklung wird kaum wahrgenommen. [...] Genauso wenig hat die kulturelle Produktion öffentliches Bewusstsein auf die Industrie, auf ihre Arbeitsweisen und ihre weitere Bedeutung zu lenken vermocht.
(Brotherstone und Manson 2007, S. 32)

Ernst Logars Engagement, unser Verständnis von Vergangenheit, Gegenwart und Zukunft zu erweitern, bestimmt sein Forschungsprojekt *Invisible Oil* über die Ölindustrie und ihre sozioökonomischen Auswirkungen auf Aberdeen, Europas „Ölhauptstadt". Das Projekt führt Logars laufende Erforschung von Orten fort, die – dem Blick der Öffentlichkeit entzogen – Zentren der bestehenden hegemonialen Ordnung sind. Logar strebt danach, diese Orte zu dokumentieren und öffentlich wahrnehmbar zu machen. Indem er ihre Unsichtbarkeit – die zu ihrer Macht beiträgt – aufdeckt, wird ihre Beziehung zu den sozioökonomischen Themen, die unsere Lebensweise bestimmen, deutlich. *Invisible Oil* zeichnet Schlüsselorte der Ölindustrie auf und ermöglicht es, die zahlreichen Ebenen, die symbolischen Bedeutungen und die ethischen Aspekte des auf fossilen Brennstoffen basierenden Energiesektors darzustellen und zu reflektieren. Die soziale Kritik ist in der Ausstellung in deren Bezug auf die Abläufe von Gewinnung, Vertrieb, Raffination und Handel stets gegenwärtig. Logar verdeutlicht, dass dieser fossile Brennstoff seit seiner Umwandlung aus den Überresten lebender Organismen vor Millionen von Jahren eine Quelle von Energie und Rohstoffen für die petrochemischen Produkte ist, von denen der Fortbestand der Industriegesellschaft in ihrer gegenwärtigen Form abhängt.

Through a glass, darkly: Visualization, revelation and reflection in Ernst Logar's *Invisible Oil*

The product serves its purpose largely unseen, finding its way into internal combustion engines, or the energy market more generally, with little perceived connection to its origins or the process that developed it. [...] Nor has cultural production been such as to draw public consciousness towards the industry, its ways of working, and its broader significance.
(Brotherstone and Manson 2007, p. 32)

Ernst Logar's commitment to expanding our understandings of the past, present and future informs *Invisible Oil,* his research project on the oil industry and its socio-economic impact on Aberdeen, Europe's 'oil capital'. The project continues Logar's ongoing investigation into spaces which, hidden from public view, are key operation centres of existing hegemonic orders. Logar strives to document these spaces, render them publicly perceptible and in dismantling their invisibility – one source of their power – make explicit their connection with the socio-economic issues affecting the ways we live. *Invisible Oil* chronicles key locations of the oil industry, facilitating visualization of and reflection on the multiple layers of symbolic meaning and ethical issues relating to the hydrocarbon energy sector. This social critique is present throughout the exhibition in its evocation of the processes of extraction, distribution, refining and retailing. Logar impresses upon us that, since its conversion from the deposition of the remains of living organisms millions of years ago, this fossil fuel is the source of energy and raw material for petrochemical products that industrialized civilization depends upon for survival in its present form.

Ausstellungsansicht 2 | Exhibition view 2

Diese allgemeine Abhängigkeit von Öl schwingt auf den tiefsten Ebenen unserer Psyche mit. Logar setzt sich nicht nur mit dieser Prämisse auseinander, sondern gibt uns auch sinnvolle Mittel zur sachkundigen Reflexion und Analyse an die Hand. Psychoanalyse und Ethnologie, zwei benachbarte Wissensgebiete, bieten einen Ausgangspunkt zur Erforschung individueller und kollektiver Ebenen des Unbewussten und der Geschichte, die es formt. Für Michel Foucault liegt der Hauptbeitrag dieser wissenschaftlichen Disziplinen darin, es Untersuchungen zu ermöglichen, „sich gezielt den unbewussten Prozessen zuzuwenden [...], die das System einer gegebenen Kultur charakterisieren" (Foucault 1974, S. 454). Wir erinnern uns vielleicht an Jungs „kollektives Unbewusstes" oder an den Begriff „Konsensus-Trance", der von dem Psychologen Charles Tart geprägt wurde, um Formen des Verleugnens in der „Peak Oil"-Debatte[1] zu bezeichnen. In diesem Wechselspiel zwischen dem „Unbewussten der Kulturen" und dem „Unbewussten von Individuen" (ebd., S. 454) verankert Logar seine Interpretation der verborgenen Prozesse der Ölindustrie und positioniert *Invisible Oil* im kritischen Diskurs. Diese Haltung entspricht Pierre Bourdieus Anspruch, dass jedes „wirklich kritische Denken [...] mit der Kritik der ökonomischen und sozialen Grundlagen kritischen Denkens beginnen" (Bourdieu und Haacke 1995, S. 79) muss.

Invisible Oil stellt in einer ganzheitlichen Ordnung die wichtigsten Variablen und Ebenen des Diskurses, die Logar während seiner Recherchen

Shared dependency on oil resonates on the most profound levels of our psyches. Logar not only tests this premise but also provides us with meaningful resources to facilitate informed reflection and analysis. Psychoanalysis and ethnology, two neighbouring forms of knowledge, offer a point of departure for the exploration of individual and collective levels of the unconscious and the history which frames it. According to Michel Foucault, the main contribution of these scientific approaches is to allow research inquiry to focus deliberately on 'the area of the unconscious processes that characterize the system of a given culture' (Foucault 1970, p. 379). We may recall the Jungian 'collective unconscious' or 'consensus trance', the phrase psychologist Charles Tart coined to characterise denial in the peak oil[1] debate. It is here – in the interplay between 'the unconscious of culture' and 'the unconscious of individuals' (ibid., p. 379) – that Logar bases his interpretation of the hidden processes of the oil industry and also his positioning of *Invisible Oil* in the critical discourse. This stance parallels Pierre Bourdieu's claim that any 'truly critical form of thought should begin with a critique of the more or less unconscious economic and social bases of critical thought itself' (Bourdieu and Haacke 1995, p. 74).

Invisible Oil introduces, in an integrated system, the main variables and levels of discourse that Logar uncovered during his research, which was conspicuously hindered by oil companies' recurring reticence to allow the artist access to the essential

1
Der Begriff „peak oil" geht auf die Recherchen des Geologen M. King Hubbert in den 1950er-Jahren zurück und bezieht sich auf jenen Punkt, an dem die weltweite Erdölförderung ihre Produktionsspitze erreicht und nach dem die Produktionsraten unwiderruflich zu sinken beginnen.

Derived from geoscientist M. King Hubbert's research in the 1950s, the term 'peak oil' refers to the point at which global petroleum extraction reaches its zenith and after which production rates begin their slide into terminal decline.

Ausstellungsansicht 3 | Exhibition view 3

aufgedeckt hat, vor. Seine Arbeit wurde auf auffällige Weise vom wiederholten Zögern der Ölfirmen, dem Künstler Zugang zu den wesentlichen Schauplätzen ihrer Industrie zu gewähren, behindert. Obwohl ihm die Dokumentation der gesamten Bandbreite wichtiger Schauplätze verweigert wurde, erreicht Logar die geplante, umfassende Konstruktion, indem er verschiedene Medien geschickt kombiniert. Die Drucke, Fotografien und Skulpturen von *Invisible Oil* sind miteinander verbunden und ergänzen einander in der Kommunikation einer provokanten Botschaft. Die Strategie regt an, was Haacke „produktiv provozieren" nennt (ebd., S. 28) – nämlich „öffentliche Debatten" (ebd., S. 28) zu fördern und Veränderung voranzutreiben, indem „kritischen Anstrengungen symbolische Wirksamkeit" (ebd., S. 28) verliehen wird, wie Bourdieu sagt. Die Arbeiten der Serie werden in benachbarten Räumen gezeigt, die durch einen schwarzen Gummivorhang geteilt sind, der zwei Ebenen desselben Systems abgrenzt. Ein Plexiglasfass auf einem Sockel in der Mitte des ersten Raumes, das ein Barrel (158,987294928 Liter) Rohöl enthält, fungiert als Achse der gesamten Ausstellung. Seine Anziehungskraft lässt alle Arbeiten von *Invisible Oil* um das Fass kreisen und ihre Bedeutung in der konkreten Referenz auf diese hervorstechende organische Substanz erlangen. Logar schlägt so ein System kritischen Denkens in Bezug auf die dringlichsten geopolitischen Fragen der Gegenwart und auf den spezifischen Kontext des Nordseeöls und die Stadt Aberdeen vor.

locales of their industry. Although he was blocked from documenting the scope of meaningful spaces, Logar accomplishes the envisaged holistic construction through the ingenious use of mixed media. The prints, photographs and sculptural pieces of *Invisible Oil* are interconnected and support one another in the communication of a provocative message. The strategy is to stimulate what Haacke calls 'productive provocation' (ibid., p. 21), that which encourages 'public debate' (ibid., p. 22) and promotes change by giving what Bourdieu calls 'critical actions a true symbolic efficacy' (ibid., p. 21). The pieces in the series are displayed in contingent rooms divided by a black rubber curtain which demarcates two levels of the same system. A perspex drum containing a barrel (158,987294928 litres) of crude oil sitting on a plinth, located in the middle of the first room, acts as the common axis for the entire exhibition. The drum's gravitational quality makes all the works of *Invisible Oil* orbit around it, attaining their meanings in strict relation to the conspicuous organic substance. Logar thus proposes a system of critical thought aimed at the most urgent geopolitical issues of the day and also at the specificity of North Sea oil and the city of Aberdeen.

folgende Doppelseite | following double page
Ausstellungsansicht 4 | Exhibition view 4

Heliport, Flughafen Aberdeen | Aberdeen Airport

Eine Kartografie von Machtverhältnissen

[...] Macht ist am wirksamsten,
wo sie am unsichtbarsten ist.
(Lukes 2005, S. 1)

Alltägliche Herrschaft wird über städtische Landschaften voller Symbole durchgesetzt, die unser Handeln und Verhalten kontrollieren. Bourdieu argumentiert, dass wir in „Metropolen [...], in denen ökonomische und symbolische Mächte konzentriert sind, Hochburgen der symbolischen Macht, die häufig auch Hochburgen der ökonomischen Macht sind", leben (Bourdieu und Haacke 1995, S. 105). Vor genau diesem Hintergrund manipuliert Logar ein „offizielles" Schild, das er neben einer BP-Leitung gesehen hat, indem er das Format kopiert und den Text subversiv durch „Invisible Oil, entry or work in this area is strictly forbidden" (Unsichtbares Öl, Zutritt oder Arbeit in diesem Gebiet streng verboten) ersetzt. Sein Schild, das für ein Übertreten von Befugnissen steht, ist am Eingang der Ausstellung plaziert, um eine unvermittelte Störung zu erzeugen „Was zum Teufel soll dieses Straßenschild hier?" – Darüber hinaus soll es uns zum Nachdenken über unsere „tatsächlichen" Möglichkeiten bewegen, auf der symbolischen Ebene zu agieren der wir uns meist unbewusst fügen. Logars Standpunkt erinnert uns daran, dass „die Ausübung von Macht verhindert, dass Menschen handeln, und manchmal sogar denken" (Lukes 2005,

A cartography of power relations

[...] power is at its most effective
when least observable.
(Lukes 2005, p. 1)

Everyday domination operates through urban landscapes filled with symbols controlling our actions and behaviour. Bourdieu argues that we live in 'cities where both economic and symbolic power are concentrated, sites of symbolic consecration which are often sites of economic power' (Bourdieu and Haacke 1995, p. 101). It is in this context that Logar manipulates an 'official' sign observed beside a BP pipeline by copying its format and subverting its caption, spawning 'Invisible Oil, entry or work in this area is strictly forbidden'. His sign, a transgression of authority, is located at the entrance of the exhibition so as to generate an abrupt disruption – 'What the hell is this road sign doing here?' – and to provoke reflection on our 'real' chances of intervening in the symbolic domain we generally accept and obey unconsciously. Logar's point reminds us that 'the exercise of power prevents people from doing, and sometimes even thinking' (Lukes 2005, p. 50). Punishment makes the development of obedience to the official demarcation of our landscapes all the more effective. Logar experienced reprimand himself, in the shape of a warning from Grampian Police, when he was

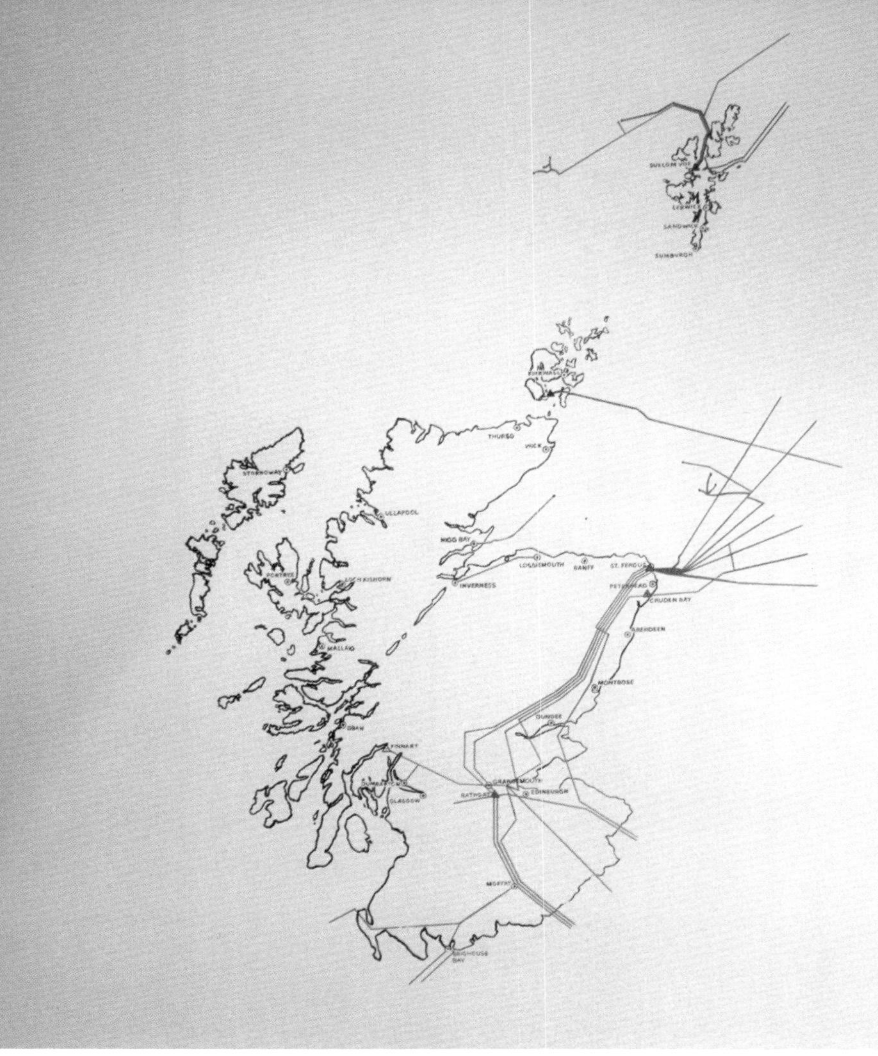

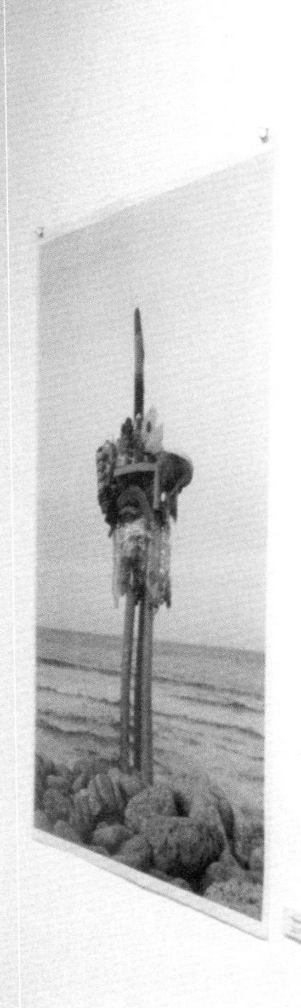

Ausstellungsansicht 5 | Exhibition view 5

S. 50). Bestrafung macht die Entwicklung von Gehorsam gegenüber den offiziellen Begrenzungen unserer Lebensräume umso wirksamer. Logar erfuhr selbst eine Zurechtweisung in Form einer Verwarnung seitens der Grampian Police, als er mit seiner Kamera zu nah am Verborgenen ertappt wurde. Er macht uns so darauf aufmerksam, was es heißt, Regeln zu befolgen, ohne deren Legitimität zu hinterfragen, und plädiert für die Entwicklung einer eigenen Praxis des Umgangs mit Macht.

Die Beziehung von Raum und Macht ist auch in der handgezeichneten Landkarte der schottischen Öl- und Gasleitungen und Raffinerien dargestellt, der man im Eingangsbereich der Ausstellung gegenübertritt. Größe ist Macht. Die Karte nimmt die ganze Wand ein – ihre vorläufige Greifbarkeit macht die Industrie als artikuliertes Ganzes sichtbar und verweist somit auf deren unterirdische Ausdehnung. Über Zeit und Raum haben wir eine Industrie festgeschrieben, die in der Folge uns festgeschrieben hat. Öl und Gas haben sowohl unseren geografischen als auch unseren geistigen Landschaften ihre Bahnen eingegraben.

caught, camera in hand, too close to the invisible. He thus calls our attention to the implications of obeying rules without questioning their legitimacy and advocates the development of our own praxis.

The relationship between space and power is also present in the hand-drawn map of Scottish oil and gas pipelines and refineries that one encounters upon entering the exhibition. Scale talks. The map dominates an entire wall – a provisional physicality giving visibility to the industry as an articulated whole and thus suggesting its subterranean outreach. Through time and space we have delineated an industry which has subsequently delineated us. Oil and gas have carved their trajectories on both our geographical and mental landscapes.

158.987294928 Litres

Enthüllung verborgener Akteure und Prozesse, die die soziale Ordnung stützen

Die Substanz, die so selten im Blickpunkt der Öffentlichkeit steht, wird in einem Plexiglasfass (Standardfassgröße: 44 Imp. gal./britische Gallonen) sichtbar. So wird zunächst ihr hoher Schadstoffgehalt und ihre visuelle Banalität mit der symbolischen Macht kontrastiert. Indem uns der Künstler mit einem Barrel konfrontiert, will er das Spektrum unserer Vorstellungen erweitern und aussagekräftigere subjektive Visualisierungen von Prozessen der Ölindustrie fördern. Die globale Dynamik dieser Industrie wird durch die Tatsache verdeutlicht, dass das hier gezeigte Rohöl, wenn auch von einer schottischen Raffinerie zur Verfügung gestellt, aus Venezuela bezogen wurde.

Der Sockel des Fasses erinnert an die Struktur eines Bohrturms und greift auch die schottische Flagge, das Andreaskreuz, auf. Gemeinsam symbolisieren Plexiglasfass und Sockel die schottische Ölindustrie. Die strategisch zentrale Position im Raum sichert ihre Machtstellung, die im Kontrast mit den Fotografien von Bohrinseln, die Logar aus weggeworfenen petrochemischen Objekten konstruiert hat, offenbart wird. Logar veranschaulicht die Unverhältnismäßigkeit zweier Parallelrealitäten: die eine dargestellt durch die reiche Bohrinsel, Quelle aller Macht, die andere durch die prekären, entrechteten und verschmutzten Attrappen. Es ist

Unveiling hidden agents and processes which prop up the social order

Showcased in a standard-sized (44 imperial/UK gallon) drum realised in perspex, the substance, so rarely in the public eye, becomes visible. The initial effect is to contrast its pollutant pungency and visual banality with its symbolic power. By confronting us with one barrel, the artist seeks to broaden our imaginary field and encourage more meaningful subjective visualizations of processes relating to an industry whose global dynamic is suggested by the fact that the crude on display here, though provided by a Scottish refinery, was in fact sourced from Venezuela.

The plinth that the drum rests upon resembles the structure of an oil rig and also replicates the Saltire. Perspex drum and plinth together symbolize the Scottish oil industry. Their strategic centricity in the room assures their position of power which becomes evident through the contrasting effect produced by the photographs of the rigs that Logar constructed with discarded petrochemical, fabricated objects. Logar confronts the disparity between two simultaneous realities, one represented by the wealthy rig, source of all power, and the other by the precarious,

Correspondence

55

kein Zufall, dass Logars Strandkonstruktionen die Namen von fünf von Aberdeens sozial am stärksten benachteiligten Gegenden tragen, während viele Bohrinseln in der Nordsee nach schottischen Vögeln benannt sind.

Logar sammelte die Objekte, die er zum Bau der in den Fotografien dokumentierten Bohrinseln verwendete, an nahe gelegenen Stränden. Die Bohrinseln wurden am Strand gebaut und dort zurückgelassen, um vom Meer weggespült zu werden und so ihre Bestandteile wieder ihrem Ursprung zurückzuführen. Das Verschwinden der temporären Bohrinseln spiegelt die Idee der Endlichkeit von fossilen Brennstoffen wider. Die Vorstellung ist verlockend, dass die Skulpturen nach einem verständnisvollen flüchtigen Blick Ausschau halten, einem Adieu der Bohrtürme und küstennahen Plattformen, welche Unsicherheit und Endlichkeit aus erster Hand erfahren. Die Piper-Alpha-Katastrophe[2] gilt hierfür als das prägnanteste Beispiel.

Den Fotografien der Bohrinsel-Skulpturen ist eine Auswahl von Logars Korrespondenz mit Ölfirmen gegenübergestellt. In dieser ersucht er um Genehmigung, Zugang zu Orten zu erhalten, die für sein Projekt essenziell sind, und diese zu dokumentieren. Der Kontakt mit der Ölindustrie bildete den Ausgangspunkt für Logars Arbeiten und beeinflusste die Entwicklung seiner künstlerischen Recherche. Seine Bemühungen um die Dokumentation dieses Vorgangs

disenfranchised and polluted mock-ups. It is no coincidence that, whereas many North Sea oil rigs are named after Scottish birds, Logar's littoral constructions bear the names of five of Aberdeen's most socially deprived areas.

Logar collected the objects he used to build the rigs, documented in the photographs, on nearby shores. These rigs, having been erected on the beach, were left to be washed away by the sea, returning the constitutive parts to their origin. A reflection on the idea of the finitude of fossil fuels is conveyed through the disappearance of these transient rigs. It is also tempting to imagine these rigs looking out to sea for a sympathetic glimpse, an adieu, from the offshore rigs and platforms which experience precariousness and finitude first-hand, the Piper Alpha disaster[2] being the most emblematic example.

Facing the photographs of the rigs is a series of printouts of Logar's correspondence with oil firms in which he requests permission to access and document essential locations for his project. Contact with the oil industry was a starting point for the artist which determined the development of his research. His efforts to record this stage are consistent with the project's emphasis on processes and systems. 'Correspondence' amounts to a representative

2
Diese küstennahe Ölkatastrophe, die als die weltweit schlimmste gilt, führte am 6. Juli 1988 zum Tod von 167 Menschen auf der Piper-Alpha-Produktionsplattform in der Nordsee.

This, commonly regarded as the world's worst offshore oil catastrophe, involved the deaths of 167 people at the Piper Alpha production platform in the North Sea on 6th July 1988.

Pumpstation | Pumping Station, Cruden Bay

setzen sich, genauso wie der Fokus auf Prozesse und Systeme, im gesamten Projekt fort. „Correspondence" umfasst eine repräsentative Auswahl des E-Mail-Verkehrs, die uns einen Eindruck der Bandbreite an Reaktionen vermittelt. Die Briefe werden nur geringfügig verändert ausgestellt; nur Namen und E-Mail-Adressen sind durchgestrichen. Die darin enthaltenen Ausflüchte durchbrechen den Kreis privater Interessen nicht und weichen möglichen Bedrohungen der systemimmanenten Ordnung aus.

Die Orte der Ölindustrie sind Orte der Macht, an denen die Handlungs- und Kontrollfähigkeit der Ölindustrie Gestalt annehmen. Wissen spielt eine wesentliche Rolle im Aufbau dieser Orte, denn um ihre Interessen und das zu wahren und zu erhalten, was Foucault als „die Seinsweise der Dinge" bezeichnet (Foucault 1974, S. 25), ist die Ölindustrie (wie jede andere Industrie der herrschenden Kultur) von Wissen abhängig. Die Begegnung mit dem gewöhnlich Verborgenen und die daraus resultierende Neubewertung von vorgefassten Meinungen haben auf uns bedeutende psychologische Auswirkungen. Indem Logar verborgene Akteure und Prozesse sichtbar macht, ermöglicht er eine einzigartige prägende Erfahrung, die komplexe kognitive Prozesse fördert, welche für unsere eigenständige Konstruktion von Realitäten und im weiteren Sinne für Erkenntnis an sich notwendig sind.

selection of e-mail communications which introduces us to a suggestive spectrum of reactions. The letters are displayed with little intervention (barring the crossing out of names and e-mail addresses) – their evasions keep the circle of private interests unbroken, evading possible threats to their order.

The spaces of the oil industry are spaces of power in the sense that they are an actualization of the oil industry's ability to act and control. Knowledge plays an essential role in the constitution of these spaces, for the oil industry (as any other industry of the dominant culture) depends on knowledge to protect its interests and maintain what Foucault calls 'the mode of being of things' (Foucault 1974, p. 25). The encounter with that which is usually hidden and the re-dimensioning of preconceptions have significant psychological effects on us. By making hidden agents and processes visible, Logar is facilitating a unique formative experience which stimulates complex cognitive processes necessary for our autonomous construction of realities and, by extension, knowledge itself.

Angehalten von der Polizei bei Cruden Bay | Stopped by the police near Cruden Bay

Doch tief unter der Oberfläche ...

Logar konfrontiert uns mit der unsichtbaren Abhängigkeit unserer Gesellschaft von Öl. Welche Auswirkungen hat diese Abhängigkeit? Unterstützt durch den strategischen Einsatz von Licht enthüllen die folgenden Arbeiten in ihrem Wechselspiel unbewusste persönliche und kollektive Prozesse.

„Derivative 01–12" zeigt Öl in seinem ursprünglichen Zustand, um den Ausgangspunkt der Umwandlungsprozesse von Rohöl in allgegenwärtige Güter, die heute als selbstverständlich gelten, hervorzustreichen und zu veranschaulichen. Für diese Serie hat Logar am Strand petrochemische Objekte gesammelt und in mit Rohöl beschichtetem Papier eingeprägt. In einem symbolischen Experiment, das seine eigene Ordnung erzeugt, versucht der Künstler die Objekte auf ihren fossilen Ursprung zurückzuführen und bringt damit Plastikmüll und Rohöl in einen in sich geschlossenen Wechselwirkungsprozess. Der Künstler greift in die Chronologie der Entstehungsgeschichte ein und bezeugt so die menschliche Rolle bei transformativen Prozessen, die in unserer Gesellschaft stattfinden, deren wir uns im Allgemeinen aber nicht bewusst sind. In symbolischem Sedimentgestein bewahrte Spuren der gegenwärtigen Zivilisation schaffen den Eindruck einer Begegnung mit vergangenem Leben, bringen die Wahrnehmung der tatsächlichen Zeitabläufe durcheinander und laden uns ein, uns selbst als Ergebnis einer Kette andauernder Veränderungen zu sehen. Die Drucke symbolisieren die unbegrenzte Möglichkeit menschlicher Kreativität im Gegensatz zur begrenzten Natur mineralischer Ressourcen und können auch als eine geistige Vorbereitung auf unsere Rückkehr zu einer einfacheren, nachhaltigeren Lebensweise gesehen werden.

But deep down below the surface...

Logar confronts us with our societies' invisible dependency on oil. What is the impact of this? In mutual interaction, the following works unveil unconscious personal and collective processes, and Logar's strategic use of light reinforces this objective.

'Derivative 01–12' presents oil in its initial state in order to acknowledge and visualize the starting point of the processes of transformation that crude oil undergoes as it transforms into the ubiquitous commodities we take for granted today. For this series, Logar embossed petrochemical objects collected onshore in paper covered in crude oil. In a symbolic experiment which creates its own order, the artist attempts to return these objects to their fossilized origin, making plastic debris and crude oil interact in a self-encompassing process. The artist intervenes in the chronology of development, attesting to the human involvement in transformative processes which take place in our society and of which we are usually unaware. Traces of contemporary civilization, preserved in symbolic sedimentary rock, create the effect of encountering that which lived in the past, dislocating the sense of real time and inviting us to see ourselves as the result of a chain of ongoing transformations. The prints are testament to the limitless possibilities of human creativity in contrast to the finite nature of mineral resources, and can also be seen as a mental preparation for our reversion to a simpler, more sustainable way of life.

folgende Doppelseite | following double page
Ausstellungsansicht 6 | Exhibition view 6

linke Seite | left page
Wellhead

Die Fotografien mit ölbeschmierten Rahmen glänzen wie (schwarzes) Gold und erinnern an verschiedene Prozesse, die vor und nach der Öffnung einer Ölreserve stattfinden. „Simulation room" und „Laboratory" sind die einzigen Fotografien von nicht-öffentlichen Räumen in der Ausstellung, während „Wellhead" Logars persönliche Visualisierung eines Bohrturms zeigt. In dieser letzten Fotografie steht ein Bohrturm buchstäblich auf dem Kopf eines Mannes. Die Konstruktion dieser Darstellung geht auf die ursprüngliche Überlegung zurück, dass unser Unbewusstes und der verborgene Inhalt des Reservoirs bereitliegen, um vom Bohrturm zutage gefördert zu werden. Im Fall des menschlichen Bewusstseins kann man dies als therapeutischen Prozess verstehen, durch den das Verdrängte zu bewusster, rationaler Erkenntnis gebracht werden kann. Die Extraktion von fossilen Brennstoffen und des Verdrängten des menschlichen Geistes kann jedoch scheitern, wenn übermäßiger Druck eine Explosion auslöst. Beim Menschen bezieht sich die Explosion auf Symptome, die vom Verdrängten, das weiterhin im Unbewussten existiert, produziert werden; im Fall der Plattform könnte sich die Explosion auf einen Gasaustritt beziehen. Allgemeiner kann „Wellhead" als Allegorie der Notwendigkeit verstanden werden, alle unsere intellektuellen Ressourcen zu nutzen (die natürlich erneuerbar sind, solange wir die Kraft zu handeln haben). Unbeständigkeit und Geheimnis kommen an die Oberfläche. Als mechanisches Werkzeug kann der Bohrlochkopf die Komplexität dessen, was er vom Geist hervorzubefördern versucht, nicht zur Gänze erfassen. Die Mechanisierung der gegenwärtigen Welt kann die tiefsten menschlichen Prozesse und ihre Manifestation in unserer Kultur nie vollständig begreifen.

The photographs with oil-smeared frames shining like (black) gold evoke various processes which take place before and after a petroleum reservoir is opened. 'Simulation room' and 'Laboratory' are the only photographs of non-public spaces in the exhibition, whilst 'Wellhead' consists of Logar's personal visualization of an oil rig. This last photograph shows a derrick literally sitting atop a man's head. The initial reflection for the construction of this representation is that our mind's unconscious and the hidden content of the reservoir are ready to be extracted through the derrick. In the case of the human mind, this can be seen as a therapeutic process, for it may bring the repressed into conscious, rational awareness. The extraction of fossil fuels and the extraction of the repressed of the human mind, however, may fail when excessive pressure provokes an explosion. In the case of human beings, the explosion refers to the symptoms produced by the repressed, which continues to exist in the unconscious and, on the oil rig, the explosion could relate to the leakage of gas. 'Wellhead', in more general terms, can be seen as an allegory for the need to use all our intellectual resources (which are naturally renewable as long as we have the power to act). Volatility and mystery emerge. The wellhead as a mechanical device cannot fully grasp the complexity of what it is trying to extract from the mind. The mechanization of the contemporary world always falls short of understanding the most profound human processes and how they manifest in our culture.

Reflecting Oil

65

„Reflecting Oil“ schließt den Kreis mit einer Darstellung der erfolgreichen Industrialisierung von Rohöl und ihrer sozialen Auswirkungen. Die Arbeit besteht aus einem großen Plexiglaskasten, durch den laufend Rohöl gepumpt wird. Durch unsere Reflexion in diesem „Spiegel“ fließenden Öls kommt es gleichzeitig zu einer Begegnung mit uns selbst sowie mit unserer Kultur – „durch einen Spiegel, in einem dunklen Wort“. Unsere Gesellschaft basiert auf dem Fließen von Öl. Millionen Barrel werden jeden Tag zur Ermöglichung unseres Lebensstils durch die Pipelines gepumpt. Logar fordert uns heraus festzustellen, wie wir uns selbst in einem Spiegel sehen, der die politischen, wirtschaftlichen und sozialen Auswirkungen dieses Kreislaufs vereint. Die von uns geschaffenen Waren und Güter prägen uns, bestimmen sie doch unsere Lebensgewohnheiten auf eine Art, wie wir sie selten wahrnehmen. „Reflecting Oil“ macht Rohöl und seine symbolische Bewegung sichtbar. Diese Idee der Bewegung ist nicht nur wörtlich zu verstehen (als jene Bewegung, die die verschiedenen Stufen der Industrialisierung von Öl umfasst), sondern auch symbolisch, im Sinne der industriellen Absicht, zu handeln und Kontrolle auszuüben. Die von „Reflecting Oil“ vermittelte Idee der Bewegung gibt der gesamten Ausstellung eine eigene Dynamik, insofern alle Prozesse, die Logar aufdeckt, davon abhängen.

Closing the circle, ‘Reflecting Oil’ evokes the successful industrialization of crude oil and its social impact. It consists of a large perspex box through which crude oil is continuously pumped. Seeing ourselves reflected in this mirror of moving oil – ‘in a glass, darkly’ – concerns encountering ourselves and our culture together. Our society is founded on the movement of oil. Millions of barrels are pumped through pipelines every day to make our lifestyles possible. Logar challenges us to discover how we see ourselves in a mirror which brings together the political, economic and social implications of this movement. The commodities that we have created, subsequently, create us because they govern the ways we live in ways we are rarely empowered to see. ‘Reflecting Oil’ makes crude oil and its symbolic movement visible. The idea of movement must be understood literally (that is, the motion making up the different stages involved in the industrialization of oil), as well as symbolically, in terms of the industrial intention to act and control. The notion of movement conveyed by ‘Reflecting Oil’ gives a distinctive dynamism to the entire exhibition, in the sense that all the processes Logar unveils depend upon it.

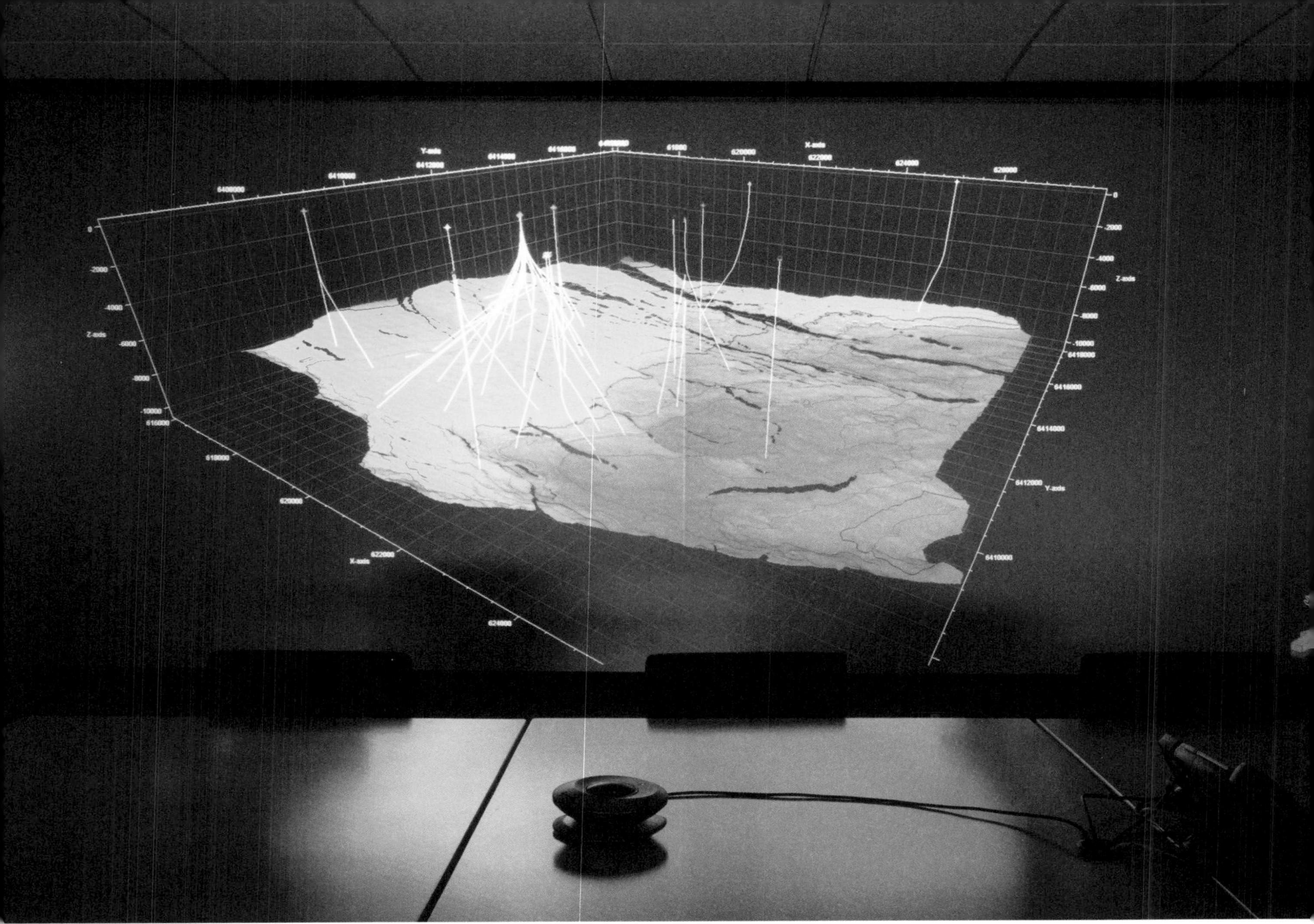

Simulationsraum | Simulation room

Der Künstler als Motor eines kritischen Rohstoffbewusstseins

Das Unvermögen, sich in die Erfahrung eines anderen einzufühlen (Einfühlung kann die Tür zum Verständnis öffnen), wird teils durch das, was ich „selektive Realität" nenne, verursacht, durch das enge Realitätsspektrum, das Menschen auswählen oder zu sehen bereit sind und/oder das ihre Kultur für sie zum „Sehen auswählt". [...] Was außerhalb des Bereichs der Konsenswahrnehmung liegt, wird „ausgeblendet".
(Anzaldúa 1990, S. xxi)

Ernst Logars *Invisible Oil* macht in einem einheitlichen System zahlreiche Faktoren, die in der Ölindustrie und in ihrer Beziehung zur Stadt Aberdeen eine Rolle spielen, sichtbar, um verborgene herrschende Machtverhältnisse zu entlarven. Das Projekt macht auch die unbewusste Dimension unserer kulturellen Konstruktionen und insbesondere der Prozesse, die die Ölindustrie ausmachen, deutlich. Logar will uns daran erinnern, dass das, was wir sehen können und was nicht, von den undurchsichtigen Machtverhältnissen unserer Kultur bestimmt ist. Dennoch ist es möglich, „symbolische Aktionsformen zu erfinden, die uns von unseren ewigen Repetitionen" befreien (Bourdieu und Haacke 1995, S. 27). Es gibt Alternativen zur „Geschichte

The artist as an agent of petroconscientization

Failure to empathize with (empathy may open the door to understanding) another's experience is due, in part, to what I call 'selective reality', the narrow spectrum of reality that human beings select or choose to perceive and/or what their culture 'selects' for them to 'see'. [...] That which is outside of the range of consensus perception is 'blanked out'.
(Anzaldúa 1990, p. xxi)

Ernst Logar's *Invisible Oil* makes visible in a unified system many variables at play in the oil industry and its relationship with the city of Aberdeen, in order to unmask hidden but overarching power. It also makes explicit the unconscious dimension of our cultural constructs and, more specifically, of the processes constituting the oil industry. Logar is at pains to remind us that what we can and cannot see is determined by the murky power relations that our culture constructs. Yet 'it is possible to invent unprecedented forms of symbolic action which will free us from our eternal repetitions' (Bourdieu and

Rohöllabor | Crude oil laboratory

des Gleichen", Foucaults Konzept der „Geschichte der Ordnung der Dinge" (Foucault 1974, S. 27). Damit wir Veränderungen in Gang setzen können, ist es wesentlich, die Ölindustrie (der selbst oft mangelnde Transparenz vorgeworfen wird) zu verstehen – vor allem in Bezug auf unseren andauernden Prozess, eine Kultur zu formen, die uns in der Folge ihrerseits prägt.

Das nahende Ende des Ölzeitalters und die Erfordernisse des Klimawandels sollten Regierungen dazu bringen, nachhaltige Energiepolitiken zu implementieren um unseren Übergang zu kohlenstoffarmen Energiesystemen zu erleichtern. Noch erzählen die Stimmen der ArbeiterInnen die Geschichte des Nordseeöls; das durch die einzigartigen persönlichen und kollektiven Erfahrungen dieser Menschen gesammelte Wissen muss als Beitrag der betroffenen Bevölkerung in die globalen Energiedebatten einbezogen werden, damit diese von Bedeutung sein können *Invisible Oil* zeigt die Stadt Aberdeen sowohl in ihrer spezifischen Einzigartigkeit als auch in einem großen Ganzen. Eine kontextualisierte Kritik, die von innen ausgeht, sollte in der Entwicklung des notwendigen kritischen Diskurses, der sowohl subjektiv als auch objektiv verantwortungsvolles, eigenständiges,

Haacke 1995, p. 20). There are alternatives to 'the history of the Same', Foucault's conceptualization of 'the history of the order imposed on things' (Foucault 1974, p. 27). Understanding of the oil industry (itself frequently accused of lacking transparency) as regards our ongoing process of making a culture which subsequently makes us is essential for our engagement in transformative action.

The fast-approaching end of the Oil Age and the exigencies of climate change ought to compel governments to implement sustainable energy policies which facilitate our transition to low-carbon energy systems. Protagonist voices are still telling the history of North Sea oil; the knowledge conveyed by these people's unique personal and collective experiences needs to inform the engagement of local communities in the global energy debate if it is to be meaningful. *Invisible Oil* presents a city, Aberdeen, in its unique specificity as well as in the bigger picture. A contextualized critique emanating from within should have a hand in developing the critical discourse needed to underpin responsible, autonomous local action both subjectively and

Tillydrone, Aberdeen

lokales Handeln unterstützt, eine Rolle spielen. Darüber hinaus trägt *Invisible Oil* dazu bei, eine Grundlage für die Einbindung der Geschichte der Nordsee in unser Verständnis von Großbritanniens Platz in der Welt zu schaffen.

Mittlerweile gibt es mehrere Versuche, das öffentliche Bewusstsein hinsichtlich der Frage von Aberdeens Zukunft in der Zeit des „Übergangs zur Postölwirtschaft", so Colin Campbell und Jean Laherrère (Campbell und Laherrère 1998, S. 83), zu stärken – auch was den potenziellen Beitrag von Kultur und Kunst zum kreativen Überdenken der entstehenden Herausforderungen angeht. Es besteht eine kollektive Notwendigkeit, diese Bemühungen zu artikulieren und zu tragen. Das labile neoliberale Wirtschaftsmodell als Ordnungsachse der Gesellschaft zeigt, dass wir auf lange Sicht in die Menschen und ihre intellektuellen Ressourcen investieren müssen, damit die Wirtschaft in den Dienst des Allgemeinwohls gestellt werden kann.

collectively. Moreover, *Invisible Oil* contributes to setting the grounds for the incorporation of the history of the North Sea into our understanding of Great Britain's place in the world.

Several efforts are being made of late to raise public awareness about Aberdeen's future, during what Colin Campbell and Jean Laherrère have called 'the transition to the post-oil economy' (Campbell and Laherrère 1998, p. 83) and the potential contribution that culture and the arts can make in the creative rethinking of the emergent challenges. There is a collective need to articulate and give sustainability to these efforts. The ongoing destabilization of the neoliberal economic model as the ordering axis for society demonstrates that we need to invest in our people and their intellectual resource, in a real long-term investment which can anchor the economy for the sake of the common good.

Wellheads Industrial Estate, Dyce, Aberdeen

Bibliografie | Bibliography

Anzaldúa, Gloria. (Hg./ed.). *Making Face, Making Soul.*
Haciendo Caras: *Creative and Critical Perspectives by Feminists of Color.*
San Francisco: Aunt Lute Foundation Press 1990.

Bourdieu, Pierre, Haacke, Hans. *Freier Austausch. Für die Unabhängigkeit der Phantasie und des Denkens.* Frankfurt am Main: S. Fischer Verlag 1995/*Free Exchange*. Cambridge: Polity Press 1995.

Brotherstone, Terry, Manson, Hugo 'North Sea Oil, its Narratives and its History: an Archive of Oral Documentation and the Making of Contemporary Britain', in: *Northern Scotland*, 27 (2007), S. 15–41/ pp. 15–41.

Campbell, Colin J., Laherrère, Jean H. 'The End of Cheap Oil', in: *Scientific American*, Vol. 278, No. 3, März 1998, S. 78–83/ pp. 78–83.

Foucault, Michel. *Die Ordnung der Dinge. Eine Archäologie der Humanwissenschaften (Les mots et les choses).* Aus dem Französischen von Ulrich Köppen. Frankfurt am Main: Suhrkamp 1974/The Order of Things: An Archaeology of the Human Sciences. London: Tavistock Publications 1970.

Lukes, Steven. *Power: A Radical View.* London: Palgrave Macmillan 2005.

73

Anhang

Appendix

ConocoPhillips (U.K.) Limited
Rubislaw House
Anderson Drive
Aberdeen AB15 6FZ
Tel: 01224 205000
Fax: 01224 205222

21 July 2008

Mr Ernst Logar
Peacock Visual Arts
21 Castle Street
Aberdeen
AB11 5BQ

Dear Mr Logar

We received your recent letter concerning support for a forthcoming art project entitled 'Non Public Spaces'.

We read your proposal with interest but regret that we are unable to assist on this occasion.

Yours sincerely

Public Affairs Co-ordinator

Von: <@nynas.com>
Betreff: Re: Photo request
Datum: Mo, 21.07.2008, 15:26
An: invisible_oil@logar.co.at

Dear Ernst,

thank you for the e-mail. I would like to discuss the content with you - please call me.

Our refinery in Dundee is unusual, as we do not use crude oil from the North Sea - our crude comes all the way from Venezuela. This is because our main product is bitumen, used in road construction, rather than gasoline. This may not fit with your project aim, but only you can decide that.

I tried to ring the number you gave me, but the gallery is closed on Mondays.

I hope to hear from you soon.

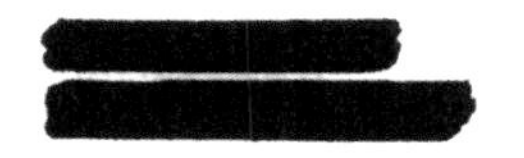

Nynas UK AB
East Camperdown Street
DD1 3LG Dundee
Tel. +44-1-382
Dir. +44-1-382
Fax +44-1-382
Mobile +
@nynas.com
http://www.nynas.com

invisible_oil@logar.co.at

21/07/2008 10:44

To
cc
Subject Photo request

Dear Mr.

I am writing to enquire about support for an art project, entitled 'Non Public Spaces'.
I am an Austrian artist living and working in Aberdeen where I have been awarded a residency at Peacock Visual Arts. The project addresses the public importance of the oil industry in Scotland.

In my exhibition at Peacock Visual Arts this coming October I will show important locations of the oil industry. I would like to seek permission to photograph the main
control room of Dundee refinery.

This project is concerned with spaces that are not in the public domain and with people's perception of them. The sites I have chosen have a special political, economic or social meaning and, as a rule, are not accessible to the public.

So far, I have documented different locations in Vienna, Paris, London, Rome and New York; for example, the office of Bureau International des Poids et Mesures (Determination of the Worldtime), the art storage areas of the Centre Pompidou and the Louvre, the main vault of the Austrian National Bank (Österreichische Nationalbank), the newsroom of BBC London, the arms depot of the Austrian Federal Police Headquarters and a number of other important non-public spaces (see enclosed photos). In addition to the photographs, there will be a theoretical text about the project as a whole and some documentation of the working process on video.

Von: [redacted]<[redacted]@marathonoil.com>
Betreff: RE: Photo request
Datum: Mi, 23.07.2008, 14:19
An: invisible_oil@logar.co.at

Thank you for your interest in Marathon. Your photography project is impressive. Unfortunately, we will not be able to participate and must decline the opportunity.

Regards,

-----Original Message-----
From: invisible_oil@logar.co.at [mailto:invisible_oil@logar.co.at]
Sent: Monday, July 21, 2008 4:27 AM
To:
Subject: Photo request

Dear

I am writing to enquire about support for an art project, entitled 'Non Public Spaces'.
I am an Austrian artist living and working in Aberdeen where I have been awarded a residency at Peacock Visual Arts. The project addresses the public importance of the oil industry in Scotland.

In my exhibition at Peacock Visual Arts this coming October I will show important locations of the oil industry. I would like to seek permission to photograph the following locations:

- the wellhead bay of an offshore oil rig
- a laboratory where crude oil is analysed
- the conference room of your company

I will also work with crude oil as a material in my exhibition. To realise this work,
I would like to obtain a barrel of crude oil. Working in this material, which constitutes the basis of our modern civilization, is a further important level of my project. This material is the economic basis of Aberdeen and of the global economy.

The exhibition will encompass the series of photographs mentioned above. This project is concerned with spaces that are not in the public domain and with people's perception of them. The sites I have chosen have a special political, economic or social meaning and, as a rule, are not accessible to the public.

So far, I have documented different locations in Vienna, Paris, London, Rome and New York; for example, the office of Bureau International des Poids et Mesures (Determination of the Worldtime), the art storage areas of the Centre Pompidou and the Louvre, the main vault of the Austrian National Bank (Österreichische Nationalbank), the newsroom of BBC London, the arms depot of the Austrian Federal Police Headquarters and a number of other important non-public spaces (see enclosed photos). In addition to the photographs, there will be a theoretical text about the project as a whole and some documentation of the working process on video.
If you were to support this exhibition by providing the crude oil, appropriate credit, thanks and acknowledgement would be prominently featured in the project documentation. Please let me know if you, or somebody else within the company, would be available to meet me to discuss my proposal further.

Yours sincerely,

Ernst Logar

Von: [redacted]<[redacted]@oilexco.com>
Betreff: RE: Photo request
Datum: Fr, 25.07.2008, 11:54
An: invisible_oil@logar.co.at

Dear Mr Logar

Thank you for your e-mail detailing your upcoming project at Peacock Visual Arts. Having discussed with our Senior VP, I am sorry to advise Oilexco is unable to help in this instance. I can, however, advise that we use Core Laboratories in Aberdeen to analyse our crude and they may be able to assist in your second request to photograph a lab.

Wishing you success in achieving your aims.

Kind regards

[redacted]

Management Assistant

-----Original Message-----
From: invisible_oil@logar.co.at [mailto:invisible_oil@logar.co.at]
Sent: 23 July 2008 23:55
To: [redacted]
Subject: Photo request

Dear Ms. [redacted]

I am writing to enquire about support for an art project, entitled 'Non Public Spaces'. I am an Austrian artist living and working in Aberdeen where I have been awarded a residency at Peacock Visual Arts. The project addresses the public importance of the oil industry in Scotland.

In my exhibition at Peacock Visual Arts this coming October I will show important locations of the oil industry. I would like to seek permission to photograph the following locations of your company:

Von: " <@chevron.com>
Betreff: RE: Photo request - appendix
Datum: Mo, 28.07.2008, 09:59
An: invisible_oil@logar.co.at

Hi Ernst

I'm afraid the day trip flights are fully booked until November so we will be unable to accommodate your request.

Apologies

-----Original Message-----
From: invisible_oil@logar.co.at [mailto:invisible_oil@logar.co.at]
Sent: 25 July 2008 19:03
To:
Subject: RE: Photo request - appendix

Hi ,

yes my request involves going offshore personally.

Best regards, Ernst

> Hi Ernst
>
> Thanks for getting in touch.
>
> Would your request involve you going offshore personally?
>
> Thanks
>
>
>
>
>
> -----Original Message-----
> From: invisible_oil@logar.co.at [mailto:invisible_oil@logar.co.at]
> Sent: 24 July 2008 09:16
> To:
> Subject: Photo request - appendix
>
>
>
> Dear ,
>
> I didn´t send you my contact:
>
> Ernst Logar
> Peacock Visual Arts
> 21 Castle Street
> Aberdeen AB11 5BQ
> t: 01224-639539
> f: 01224-627094
> invisible_oil@logar.co.at
> www.logar.co.at
>
>
> Yours sincerely,
>
> Ernst Logar
>
>
>
>

Von: <@gbr.apachecorp.com>
Betreff: RE: RE:RE: Photo request
Datum: Do, 31.07.2008, 16:49
An: "'invisible_oil@logar.co.at'" <invisible_oil@logar.co.at>

Ernst

Please can you contact Mr next week on and he will explain the reason.

-----Original Message-----
From: invisible_oil@logar.co.at [mailto:invisible_oil@logar.co.at]
Sent: 31 July 2008 15:40
To:
Subject: RE:RE: Photo request

Dear

Many thanks for your reply. I regret that you cannot support my project.
However, an important aspect of my artistic project 'Non Public Spaces' is the communication process with the companies and institutions.
I would therefore like to know for what reasons your company is unable to support my request. I would be grateful for your feedback.

With thanks
and my best regards, Ernst Logar

Ernst Logar
Peacock Visual Arts
21 Castle Street
Aberdeen AB11 5BQ
t: 01224-639539
f: 01224-627094
http://www.logar.co.at

> Ernst
>
> Re E-Mail - 20 July
>
> Unfortunately we are unable to help on this occasion. We thank you
> for your interest in Apache North Sea.
>
>
>
> -----Original Message-----
> From: invisible_oil@logar.co.at [mailto:invisible_oil@logar.co.at]
> Sent: 20 July 2008 13:32
> To:
> Subject: Photo request
>
> Dear
>
> I am writing to enquire about support for an art project, entitled
> 'Non Public Spaces'.
> I am an Austrian artist living and working in Aberdeen where I have
> been awarded a residency at Peacock Visual Arts. The project addresses
> the public importance of the oil industry in Scotland.
>
> In my exhibition at Peacock Visual Arts this coming October I will
> show important locations of the oil industry. I would like to seek
> permission to photograph the following locations of Apache North Sea Limited:
>
> - the wellhead bay of an offshore oil rig
> - a laboratory where crude oil is analysed
>

31st July 2008

Ernst Logar
Peacock Visual Arts
21 Castle Street
Aberdeen
AB11 5BQ

Dear Mr Logar

Support for an Art Project

Further to your letter of 23rd July 2008 regarding the above subject, it is with regret that Venture Production plc cannot grant you permission to photograph the locations as detailed in your letter and unfortunately, cannot supply you with a barrel of crude oil.

We hope that your project is successful and wish you the best of luck for the future.

Yours Sincerely

PA to Chief Executive

Registered in Scotland No: 169182
Trading Address: Kings Close, 62 Huntly Street, Aberdeen AB10 1RS
Tel: +44 (0) 1224 Fax: +44 (0) 1224
Registered Office: 34 Albyn Place, Aberdeen AB10 1FW

Von: <@talisman.co.uk>
Betreff: Your request
Datum: Di, 5.08.2008, 11:12
An: invisible_oil@logar.co.at

Good morning Ernst

Many thanks for your letter regarding your "Non Public Spaces" project, and for considering Talisman Energy as a potential supporter of the exhibition.

Unfortunately, on this occasion, Talisman is unable to assist with access to offshore or its control rooms at Nigg and Flotta, or with the mathematical 'barrel' of crude oil. As such, perhaps another operator might be able to assist.

I wish you every success with the exhibition and look forward to visiting it.

Best regards

Talisman Energy (UK) Limited
163 Holburn Street
Aberdeen
AB10 6BZ

Tel: 01224
Email: @talisman.co.uk

Anhänge:

untitled-1	
Größe:	0.9 k
Typ:	text/plain

Shell U.K. Limited
Communications
1 Altens Farm Road
Nigg
Aberdeen
AB12 3FY
United Kingdom
Tel +44 (0) 1224 88
Fax +44 (0) 1224 88
Email @shell.com
Internet http://www.shell.com/eandp

Mr Ernst Logar
Peacock Visual Arts
21 Castle Street
Aberdeen
AB11 5BQ

12 August 2008

Dear Mr Logar

Many thanks for your letter requesting support for your art project within Peacock.

Much as we appreciate the difficulties in getting the access you need for your project, I'm afraid that we are unable to offer any support.

As you can imagine, we do receive a large number of requests which means that even some of the most interesting have to be declined.

I would however, like to wish you all the very best in the areas from alternative sources.

Yours sincerely
Shell U.K. Limited

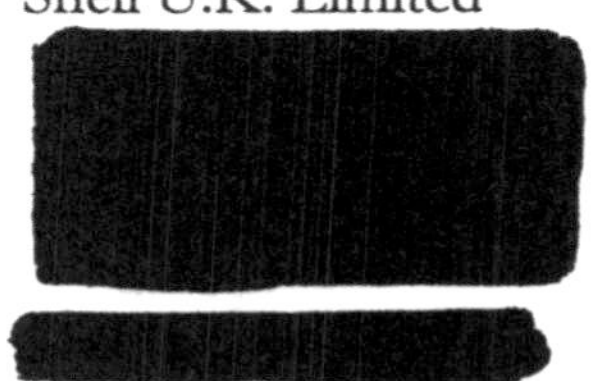

Community Relations

Shell U.K Limited
Registered in England number 140141
Registered office Shell Centre London SE1 7NA
VAT reg number GB 235 7632 55

Von: [redacted]@gdfbdrilling.com>
Betreff: RE: Photo request
Datum: Mi, 13.08.2008, 14:47
An: invisible_oil@logar.co.at

Ernst,

I appreciate your interest in wanting to capture the essence of GDF Britain and promoting the company, but we are not yet in a position to supply you with the requirements as we are only planning to drill our first oil well in the UK sector at the end of this year.
I would suggest that you should try some of the other oil companies who are producing oil at this time as they will be better placed to assist you.

All the very best in your project,

Regards,

Base Manager/Drilling Superintendent

GDF Britain Ltd.
Regus,
1, Berry Street,
Aberdeen.
AB25 1HF
Reception - +44 (0)1224
Direct - +44 (0)1224
Mobile - +44 (0)
@gdfbdrilling.com

-----Original Message-----
From: invisible_oil@logar.co.at [mailto:invisible_oil@logar.co.at]
Sent: 13 August 2008 11:15
To: @gdfbdrilling.com
Subject: Photo request

Dear Mr.

I am writing to enquire about support for an art project, entitled 'Non Public Spaces'.I am an Austrian artist living and working in Aberdeen where I have been awarded a residency at Peacock Visual Arts. The project addresses the public importance of the oil industry in Scotland.

In my exhibition at Peacock Visual Arts this coming October I will show important locations of the oil industry. I would like to seek permission to photograph the following locations of Gaz de France Britain:

- the wellhead bay of an offshore oil or gas rig
- a laboratory where crude oil or gas is analysed
- an immersion room, where exploration is simulated

I will also work with crude oil as a material in my exhibition. To realise this work, I would like to obtain a barrel of crude oil. Working in this material, which constitutes the basis of our modern civilization, is a further important level of my project. This material is the economic basis of Aberdeen and of the global economy.

The exhibition will encompass the series of photographs mentioned above. This project is concerned with spaces that are not in the public domain and with people's perception of them. The sites I have chosen have a special political, economic or social meaning and, as a rule, are not accessible to the public.

So far, I have documented different locations in Vienna, Paris, London, Rome and New York; for example, the office of Bureau International des Poids et Mesures (Determination of the Worldtime), the art storage areas

Von: " <@stavanger.oilfield.slb.com>
Betreff: Fwd: RE: RE: Photo request
Datum: Di, 19.08.2008, 07:34
An: invisible_oil@logar.co.at

Hello,
I have received a positive response from our PVT analysis lab in Aberdeen, to your request to photograph a laboratory, however they say they would need to be able to check which photos are being used to make sure they don't show anything confidential. The other problem is that there are building works going on at the moment there, so it's a bit messy outside, but inside the lab should be ok.

Please contact , Facilities Administrator, OilPhase at: @aberdeen.oilfield.slb.com to arrange a suitable time.

I haven't done anything about the London visit yet, as I believe you were going to send me some suitable dates?

Regards,

-----Original Message-----
From: invisible_oil@logar.co.at [mailto:invisible_oil@logar.co.at]
Sent: Friday, August 08, 2008 11:24 AM
To: @aberdeen.oilfield.slb.com
Subject: [Fwd: Photo request]

Dear

As just discussed over the phone, please find below the email from artist Ernst Logar. We would be truly grateful for any assistance you may be able to lend to this project.

Warm regards,
Monika Vykoukal

Curator
Peacock visual arts
21 Castle Street
Aberdeen AB11 5BQ
t 01224 639 539
www.peacockvisualarts.com
Tue-Sat 9.30am - 5.30pm
Admission Free

registered in Scotland
number SC 56235
charity number 14840

---------------------- Ursprüngliche Nachricht ------------------------
Betreff: Photo request
Von: invisible_oil@logar.co.at
Datum: Mi, 30.07.2008, 10:51
An: @aberdeen.oilfield.slb.com

Dear Mr.

I am writing to enquire about support for an art project, entitled 'Non Public Spaces'. I am an Austrian artist living and working in Aberdeen where I have been awarded a residency at Peacock Visual Arts. The project addresses the public importance of the oil industry in Scotland.

In my exhibition at Peacock Visual Arts this coming October I will show

Von: "[redacted] <[redacted]@intertek.com>
Betreff: RE: Photo request
Datum: Mi, 20.08.2008, 15:09
An: invisible_oil@logar.co.at

Ernst,

We are checking on the legal ramifications of having you in for a photo shoot. Please allow me some time to get the Headquarters to look at it.

I have said it would be good publicity for us, but am awaiting approval. What kind of time frame are you looking at completion of this project? It might be necessary for you to come in next week to see my boss and state your case.

I'll be in touch.

Best Regards,

Intertek - Analytical Services Division
Tel: (01224)

Wellheads Crescent,
Wellheads Industrial Estate
Dyce, Aberdeen AB21 7GA
Mob.
Fax: 01224 722894

-----Original Message-----
From: invisible_oil@logar.co.at [mailto:invisible_oil@logar.co.at]
Sent: 20 August 2008 08:15
To:
Subject: RE: Photo request

Dear

thank you very much for your support! I will fulfill all the issues!

Best regards, Ernst Logar

> Ernst,
>
> I will be in touch once I speak to my boss concerning this. There may
> be some issues concerning the oil you want, what exactly you want to
> do with it and how will it be disposed of once you are done with your
> project, but let's see.
>
> Best Regards,
>
>
>
>
> Intertek - Analytical Services Division
> Tel: (01224)
>
> Wellheads Crescent,
> Wellheads Industrial Estate
> Dyce, Aberdeen AB21 7GA
> Mob.
> Fax: 01224 722894
>
> -----Original Message-----
> From: invisible_oil@logar.co.at [mailto:invisible_oil@logar.co.at]
> Sent: 18 August 2008 13:23
> To:

Von: [redacted] <[redacted]@Subsea7.com>
Betreff: RE: Photo
Datum: Mo, 25.08.2008, 12:13
An: invisible_oil@logar.co.at

Hi Ernst,

The photo is fine, thank you very much.

The description of the photo should be of an 'Air Decompression Chamber'.

I have attached our logo in a couple of formats and I will post you one of our brochures as I promised.

For some more info about offshore diving, try this link:
http://www.imca-int.com/documents/careers/IMCA-Careers-id-Diving.pdf.
The IMCA website is a good source of information on the marine industry, including the subsea oil and gas sector. You could also try Wikipedia and search for 'saturation diving' if you want more information.

I'll let you know if there is an opportunity to get on one of our vessels, however as I mentioned we don't get many opportunities to get on them.

Kind Regards,
[redacted]

-----Original Message-----
From: invisible_oil@logar.co.at [mailto:invisible_oil@logar.co.at]
Sent: 25 August 2008 09:46
To: [redacted]
Subject: Photo

Dear [redacted]

Thank you very much for your support!
I am sending you the photo of the compression room, so you an check and approve it. Please send me the logo of Subsea 7, so I will put it on the supporter panel.
It would be great if I could take some photos of facilities at one of your
vessels at Peterhead.
Please let me know.

Thanks a lot and
Regards, Ernst

Ernst Logar
Peacock Visual Arts
21 Castle Street
Aberdeen AB11 5BQ
t: 01224-639539
f: 01224-627094
invisible_oil@logar.co.at
http://www.logar.co.at

> Hi Ernst,
>
>
>
> I can confirm the details of your visit to our Subsea 7 Greenwell site
> next week.
>

Marathon House
Rubislaw Hill
Anderson Drive
Aberdeen AB15 6FZ
Telephone: +44 (0)1224 803000
Facsimile: +44 (0)1224 803190

20 October 2008

Mr Ernst Logar
Peacock Visual Arts
21 Castle Street
ABERDEEN
AB11 5BQ

Dear Mr Logar

ART PROJECT – REQUEST FOR SUPPORT

With reference to your letter dated 27 August 2008 to Ms [redacted] I regret to inform you that we are unable to provide support towards your art project on this occasion.

Requests for support for so many worthwhile projects number more and more each year and whilst we do our best to help as many local charities and community initiatives as possible, many more are unfortunately disappointed.

I am sorry we are unable to help.

Yours sincerely
MARATHON OIL U.K., LTD.

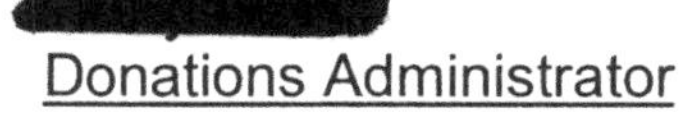

Donations Administrator

Marathon Recycles

Biografien

Karin Kneissl ist seit 1998 freischaffend als Lehrbeauftragte (Wien, Beirut etc.) und Publizistin tätig. Zuvor wirkte sie zehn Jahre im diplomatischen Dienst der Republik Österreich. Sie lehrt und schreibt u. a. zum Nahen Osten, zum Völkerrecht und zur Geopolitik der Energie. 2008 erschien die 2. Auflage ihres Buches „Der Energiepoker“ (München, FinanzBuch Verlag). Sie studierte Jus und Arabisch in Wien, Jerusalem, Amman und Washington. In ihrer Dissertation beschäftigte sie sich mit dem „Grenzbegriff der Konfliktparteien im Nahen Osten“.

Ernst Logar lebt und arbeitet in Wien. Er studierte Experimentelle Gestaltung an der Kunstuniversität Linz und Transmediale Kunst an der Universität für angewandte Kunst Wien. Neben seiner Tätigkeit als Leiter des Bereichs Medientechnik in der Generali Foundation Wien von 1995 bis 2003 beginnt er sich bereits ab 1995 mit den Medien Fotografie, Film und Skulptur sowie räumlichen installativen Arbeiten auseinanderzusetzen. In seiner Arbeit *Non Public Spaces* (1998–2011) thematisiert Ernst Logar bestehende Machtverhältnisse wie auch zeitgeschichtliche und soziokulturelle Phänomene. Die Dekonstruktion von gesellschaftlichen Mechanismen und historischen Gemeinplätzen – oftmals auch angelehnt an seine eigene Biografie wie in den Arbeiten *Den Blick hinrichten* (2004/05) und *Das Ende der Erinnerung – Kärntner PartisanInnen* (2008) – stellt einen zentralen Punkt Logars künstlerischer Praxis dar. In seinen neueren Arbeiten setzt sich Ernst Logar in *Monetary Interventions in Public Space* (2009) mit unserem heutigen Geldbegriff und in *Sustainable Transformation* (2010) mit dem Thema Nachhaltigkeit auseinander. [www.logar.co.at]

Biographies

Karin Kneissl has worked as a freelance university instructor (in Vienna, Beirut and elsewhere) and as a writer since 1998. She previously spent ten years in the diplomatic service of the Republic of Austria. She teaches and writes on topics including the Middle East, international law and the geopolitics of energy. 2008 saw the release of the second edition of her German-language book *Der Energiepoker [Energy Poker]* by the Munich-based publisher FinanzBuch Verlag. Kneissl studied law and the Arabian language in Vienna, Jerusalem, Amman and Washington. Her doctoral dissertation dealt with the ‘Diverging Concepts of Borders among the Parties in the Middle East Conflict’.

Ernst Logar lives and works in Vienna, Austria. He studied Experimental Design at the University of Fine Arts Linz and Transmedia Art at the University of Applied Arts Vienna. While employed as lead media technician at Generali Foundation between 1995 and 2003, he begins his artistic engagement with the media of photography, film and sculpture as well as spatial installation works already back in 1995. In his work *Non Public Spaces* (1998–2011) Ernst Logar engages with existing power relations as well as historical and socio-cultural phenomena. The deconstruction of social mechanisms and historical truisms – often also connected to his own biography, such as in the works *Den Blick hinrichten* (2004/05) and *The End of Remembering – Carinthian Partisans* (2008) – constitutes a central focus of Logar’s artistic practice. In his recent works, Ernst Logar has dealt with our present-day concept of money in *Monetary Interventions in Public Space* (2009) and the theme of sustainability in *Sustainable Transformation* (2010). [www.logar.co.at]

Alejandra Rodríguez-Remedi lebt als unabhängige Wissenschaftlerin in Aberdeen, Schottland, und ist Mitglied des Kollektivs New Social Art School (www.newsocialartschool.org). Sie hat in vielen Bereichen der Bildungsforschung Erfahrungen gesammelt und an einem großen innovativen Projekt zur Entwicklung alternativer Lehrpläne für berufsbildende Schulen in ihrem Heimatland Chile teilgenommen. Ihre Dissertation „Kunst als Mittel kultureller Integration: Eine chilenische Fallstudie" (The Robert Gordon University, Aberdeen 2007) befasst sich mit Identitätskonstruktionen, der (trans)formativen Dimension von Kulturproduktion, den Narrativen von Orten und radikal pluralistischer Demokratie. Auf der Suche nach kreativen Formen des Wissens hat Alejandra Rodríguez-Remedi im Rahmen der Arbeit an ihrer Dissertation poetische Kurzfilme zu machen begonnen. Zurzeit recherchiert sie zur Poetik und Didaktik des chilenischen Filmemachers Raúl Ruiz, für den sie an der University of Aberdeen gearbeitet hat.

Peter Troxler lebt in Rotterdam und arbeitet in Europa. Er hat in vielfältigen Kontexten als Produzent transdisziplinärer Projekte, Veranstaltungen, Kunstfestivals, Schauspielproduktionen und Konferenzen gearbeitet, die Kunst, Wissenschaft, Medien und die Öffentlichkeit einbezogen und integrierten. In Aberdeen gründete er die Kunstgruppe urbanNovember (2004/06), die 2005 das Projekt „Oil and the City" organisierte [http://oilandthecity.org.uk].

Ernst Ulrich von Weizsäcker. *1939, Kopräsident, International Resource Panel. Früher: Biologieprofessor, Universitätspräsident, Direktor bei der UNO, Präsident des Wuppertal Instituts, 1998–2005 MdB (SPD), Stuttgart, Vorsitzender Bundestagsumweltausschuss. 2006–2008 Leiter der kalifornischen Umwelthochschule Santa Barbara. Neuestes Buch: „Faktor fünf" (2010). [www.ernst.weizsaecker.de]

Alejandra Rodríguez-Remedi is an independent researcher based in Aberdeen, Scotland, and is affiliated with the New Social Art School collective (www.newsocialartschool.org). She is experienced in many areas of educational research and participated in a major project on alternative curricular construction for vocational schools in her native Chile. Her doctoral project, 'The arts as means of cultural integration: A Chilean case study' (awarded by The Robert Gordon University in 2007), took an interdisciplinary look at identity construction, the (trans)formative dimension of the making of culture, narratives of place and radical plural democracy. She began making poetic short films during her PhD in a search for creative ways of knowing. She is currently researching the poetics and pedagogy of Chilean filmmaker Raúl Ruiz, whom she assisted at the University of Aberdeen.

Peter Troxler lives in Rotterdam and works in Europe. He has worked, in many varied contexts, as a producer of transdisciplinary projects, events, arts festivals, drama productions and conferences including and integrating arts, academia, media and public involvement. He founded the arts collective urbanNovember (2004/06) in Aberdeen, which produced the project 'Oil and the City' [http://oilandthecity.org.uk] in 2005..

Ernst Ulrich von Weizsäcker. (*1939) is co-chair of the UN International Panel for Sustainable Resource Management. In the past, he been a professor of biology, a university president, a UN Director and President of the Wuppertal Institute; he also represented the State of Baden-Württemberg as a member of the German Bundestag (SPD) from 1998–2005, where he chaired the Environmental Committee. From 2006 to 2008 he was dean of the Bren School of Environmental Science and Management of the University of California at Santa Barbara. His latest book is entitled *Factor Five* (2010). [www.ernst.weizsaecker.de]

Impressum | Imprint

Ernst Logar, Wien | Vienna

Printed in Austria

SpringerWienNewYork is part of
Springer Science+Business Media
springer.at

Mit Unterstützung von | With support from

Konzept | Concept: Ernst Logar, Monika Vykoukal
Realisierung | Realization: Ernst Logar
Grafische Gestaltung | Graphic Design: Olaf Osten
Übersetzung | Translation: Christopher Roth, Monika Vykoukal
Lektorat | Copy editing: Wolfgang Astelbauer, Elisabeth Huber, Simon Robinson
Fotos | Photographs: Ernst Logar
Alle Fotografien und künstlerischen Arbeiten entstanden 2008 in Aberdeen und Umgebung. | All photographs and other artworks were created in and around Aberdeen in 2008.

Illustrationen | Illustrations: Ernst Logar, Olaf Osten
S. | p. 2, 3 Weltkarte | World map
S. | p. 6 Nordsee | North Sea
S. | p. 8 Naher Osten und Kaspisches Meer | Middle East and Caspian Sea

Umschlagbild | Cover Photo: *Logie* (Ernst Logar, 2008)

Druck | Printed by: Holzhausen Druck GmbH, 1140 Wien, Austria

Gedruckt auf säurefreiem, chlorfrei gebleichtem Papier – TCF
Printed on acid-free and chlorine-free bleached paper
SPIN: 80026658

Mit 57 Abbildungen, 43 in Farbe
With 57 images, 43 in color

Bibliografische Information der Deutschen Nationalbibliothek
Die Deutsche Nationalbibliothek verzeichnet diese Publikation in der Deutschen Nationalbibliografie; detaillierte bibliografische Daten sind im Internet über http://dnb.d-nb.de abrufbar.

ISSN 1866-248X
ISBN 978-3-7091-0460-6 SpringerWienNewYork

Für ihre Unterstützung danke ich
For their support I would like to thank

Brian Andrew, Emma Balkind, Terry Brotherstone, Graham Gall, Simon Glen, Lindsay Gordon, Britta Hallbauer, Michael Heaney, Caroline Kinghorn, Tom Kirk, Elisabeth Ladstätter, Katharina Ladstätter, Johanna Lettmayer, Owen Logan, Lynn Louque, Lyndsey MacDonald, Ina Mertens, Jake Molloy, Jim O'Donnell, Nadja Pakesch, Brian Ross, Stephan Scharf, John Scrimgeour, Ray Shaw, Ewan Sinclair, Danny Stroud, Steve Trueman, Neil Williamson.

Besonders dankbar bin ich Monika Vykoukal für ihre Unterstützung bei der Ausstellungs- und Buchproduktion. Michael Waight danke ich für seine Unterstützung bei der Herstellung der Rohöl-Drucke. | Special thanks to Monika Vykoukal for her support producing the exhibition and the book. Also special thanks to Michael Waight for his support producing the crude oil prints.

Die Ausstellung *Invisible Oil* wurde 2008 bei Peacock Visual Arts (www.peacockvisualarts.com) in Aberdeen realisiert. | The exhibition *Invisible Oil* was realized at Peacock Visual Arts (www.peacockvisualarts.com) in Aberdeen in 2008.

Kurator | Curator: Monika Vykoukal

folgende Doppelseite | following double page
Cruden Bay